Come Heller High Water 2

ISBN 0-9714951-0-6

Printed in the United States of America.

Cover photographs by Steve Jessmore
Design & Layout by Jamie Bully
Author Photo by Steve Kleeman

First Edition

To Marcia, without whom my life
- and ideas file -
would be far emptier

Foreword

I am frequently asked, "Why do you call your column and your books 'Come Heller High Water'? It makes no sense."

My answer is usually along the lines of, "You're right. It makes no sense whatsoever if you stop to think about it." So my advice to you is don't. (I'll pause while that sinks in.)

Besides, I had to call the book something. All the good titles for books – "The Firm," "Romeo & Juliet" and "Horton Hears a Who" – were already taken, so I did the best I could.

The origin of the name, of course, comes from the phrase "Come hell or high water," which is something my Grandma Rose used to say a lot, as in, "Young man you'd better stop torturing your sister or, come hell or high water, I'll whip you good."

I first used the phrase atop columns I wrote for CM Life, the campus newspaper at Central Michigan University. At the time, it was fashionable for columnists to title their columns with a twist on their surname, and that's the only twist I could think of other than "Go to Heller ..." which is a better reflection of what I do, but still not acceptable in most newspapers.

I've used it ever since, both on my weekly bits-and-pieces columns (none of which, oddly enough, you'll find in here due to their topical nature) and for this, the second in a series of what I suppose are my greatest hits. By that I mean that the columns you see herein are the ones most requested by people who contact me looking for reprints.

If you don't see your favorite, don't worry.

Come Heller high water, I'll put them in the next book.

Andrew Heller

Contents

If I Were King

Wedded Bliss

The Young and the Restless

It's a Mad, Mad, Mad, Mad World

Moon & Friends

Of Jocks and Jerks

So You Wanna Be a Yooper

Me, Myself and I

If I Were
King

Thexy?
How about
sthupid?

I said to the clerk at the local stop 'n' rob, "Excuse me, but do you have AAA batteries?"

Her response startled me.

"Thure!" she said pertly.

"Theyah ovah theyah."

"Excuse me?" I said.

"Ovah theyah. Neckth to thuh film. Thee it?"

This time I looked at her as she spoke and sure enough, she had a large silver tongue stud.

Dealing with Pierced America is one of the most annoying trends of the past few years. Half the waitresses who serve me now have tongue studs. I hate it.

"What (click) kin (click-click) I git (clickety-clack) youse?"

It puts me off my feed every time. Just the thought of something metal stuck through my tongue makes me want to gag.

Plus, there's the worry that if I am served food by someone with 14 earrings, a nose ring and a pierced tongue that they're likely to spit in my food if I stare.

But how can you not? Maybe it's the parent in me, but every time I encounter some young person with a pierced anything, I want to scream, "What the hell were you thinking?"

First of all, it can't be any fun to have some swarthy, tattooed stranger jab a needle through your flesh, especially your tongue. Your tongue is ... well, for God's sake, it's your

tongue! Tongues shouldn't be pierced. They just shouldn't.
I asked the clerk whether the pain and the expense was worth it and she said, "Thure!"

Sure, she was lisping because she'd only recently been pierced and her tongue was still a bit thwollen, er, I mean, swollen. But it was all worth it, she said, because, as she put it, "It lookth cool."

No, it doesn't. It lookth sthupid. All pierced body parts look stupid, except for ears. I ran into a kid at the local college where I work out who was wearing a silver ring in his eyebrow. It didn't make him look cool. It made him look like a human hand grenade. The temptation to pull his pin and lob his head at an enemy bunker was almost irresistible.

Then there was a young female student at the college where I teach. She had a belly-button ring.

"Why did you do that?" I asked.

"I dunno," she shrugged. "My boyfriend thinks it's sexy."

No, it's not. That's the least sexy thing I can think of. A ring in your belly doesn't look alluring. It looks, I dunno, like a drain plug or something. Yank it and out goes your spinal fluid.

Look, I understand what's going on here. The past decade has been relatively prosperous in America. Kids have little to rebel against. So they've latched onto: A) the most extreme and ridiculous thing they could think of, B) the thing most likely to tick off their parents.

Teens need to rebel. That's how it is. But I wonder if these human pin cushions have considered the future?

The future will happen, you know. There will come a day when you're old (you know, in your 30s or 40s) and you will have kids yourself and you'll be looking at photo albums and you'll come across a few shots of you with more gleaming metal affixed to you than a '57 Buick.

And your kids will say, "Mommy, daddy, can WE get a nose ring? Can we get a tongue stud? You know, like you."

That's when you, too, will think, "What the hell WAS I thinking?" And you will rue your silly, pierced past.

Thorry, but it's true.

—July 24, 2000

A cellphone law we can live with

I was a half-mile into the woods when I heard the most peculiar sound from beyond a bend in the trail up ahead.

It was a sharp, high-pitched chirping, not unlike a summer cicada vibrating the flapper in its belly, and I was eager to see what kind of a bio-mutant whopper could produce that kind of volume.

Then as I drew nearer I heard another sound, a far shriller, more obnoxious sound.

"Hi, Bill! It's Joe! About that Johnson deal, what I was thinking was ..."

Cellphone. I hate cellphones. They are everywhere. It's the favorite appendage of modern man.

The one to which this phone was attached was of the loud, oblivious, middle-aged variety, the worst kind. Fancy watch. Fancy Yuppie clothing. Fancy trophy wife (complete with halter top) bobbing in a speedboat in the river behind him.

He had apparently clambered on shore to make his call so his wife and their friends, Biff and Suzy, could continue their own loud conversations undisturbed.

How thoughtful of him.

Of course he forgot that his noisy deal-making might be an affront to God and nature, not to mention me.

But such things are piffle to modern man. To modern man, the world is his phone booth and if that bothers you, well, then tough luck. Here's two bits, call someone who gives a damn.

That's why I'm all in favor of what New York state has done. It has become the first state in the union to bar motorists from using hand-held phones while driving.

Critics of the law, which is expected to be copied across the land, moan that the government has no business butting into their business.

"You can't legislate everything!" one such moan goes. "If they're going to legislate car phones because they're distracting to drivers, why not go after car stereos, too?"

It's a good point. There are dozens of distractions to drivers - bratty kids, dropped cassettes, sloppy cheeseburgers. I've seen people read newspapers and apply makeup while steering. I've seen people making out, using laptops, playing harmonicas.

Certainly, all of these things can cause accidents just as surely as someone chatting up another businessman on his cellphone.

But the law says you can't drive drunk, so what's the difference between that and banning the devices that make people drive as if they're drunk? None that I see. If your family is wiped out by a jerk who's busy ordering a pizza on his cellphone, are you going to feel better that at least the driver wasn't a victim of government intervention?

I doubt it. Besides, for once the slippery slopers - those predictable dullards who always claim that one restriction inevitably leads to another - might actually turn out to be right in this case. And what a wonderful thing that would be.

If states everywhere enforce phone civility in cars, maybe they'll do it elsewhere as well. Theaters, malls, golf courses, funerals, forests. And if they make cellphone use illegal in those places, maybe that will ultimately lead to the sort of phone legislation we truly need – an obnoxious twit law.

To save our lawmakers the trouble, I have taken the liberty of authorizing just such a law. It goes: "Any use of a cellphone in a manner or location that I find personally objectionable shall entitle me to legally snatch said phone and cram it where the sun don't shine."

They might want to put that in legalese, though.

– July 15, 2001

Filling gaps in the patients' Bill of Rights

It's nice, I suppose, that Congress is set to pass a patients' Bill of Rights.

The bill, once law, would let people sue their HMOs, which is something you can't do currently.

That's only right. If your HMO says it'll only pay to have one of your three clogged arteries cleared out, provided you say pretty please, you should be able to sue, don't you think?

But there are problems. For one, the way the bill is written, you'll be able to sue, but the HMO won't have to pay any more than $1.5 million in punitive damages, even if the doctors amputate your head instead of your right big toe.

What's $1.5 million to an HMO? Nothing. They make that much every 14 seconds.

So, really, when an HMO is in the wrong, what's to get it to change? Nothing. Thank your friendly neighborhood Republican president for that.

There are other problems. The framers of the bill completely overlooked numerous common patient concerns. I have taken the liberty of filling in the gaps.

In my patients' Bill of Rights:

1. Doctors immediately and forevermore shall subscribe to no fewer than 10 general-interest magazines and keep said magazines in their waiting rooms no longer than two weeks after the month of their publishing. "Trout Fishing Unlimited" and "Fat-Free Cooking for Left-Handed Atheists" shall not be construed to be general-interest magazines for purposes of this bill.

2. Waiting room waits shall be limited to no more than 15 minutes. Come on, we're sick here, OK? Any wait longer than 15 minutes shall entitle said patient to a 50 percent-off coupon, redeemable at a future doctor's office visit.

3. Doctors shall end the practice of moving patients from the waiting room to an examining room, only to have them sit there for another half hour. Patients shall only be moved into an examining room if the doctor is there and waiting. We, after all, are the customers. It is not our privilege to see you. It is YOUR privilege to see us. (Remember, we're the ones who pay for your BMW.)

4. No doctor shall lecture us on the importance of eating right, exercising and not smoking if said doctor is a fat, inactive, chain-smoking slob.

5. Doctors shall not utter the words "This won't hurt" or "This will only sting a little" when, in fact, they know it's gonna hurt like hell.

6. If we are sick enough or hurt enough to go to a hospital emergency room, said emergency room personnel shall not: A) Make us fill out six truckloads of paperwork - for purposes of this bill the rule shall be "help first, forms later"; B) Make us sit in the waiting room for six hours bleeding all over the Formica. If we come to the emergency room, to us it's an "emergency." That means hurry up.

7. Upon admittance to a hospital, patients shall not be issued cheap cotton or paper gowns that show off our backsides to the world, as most of us spend our lives hiding our backsides for a reason.

8. Hospital nurses shall be banned from waking patients 12 times a night in order to check fluids or temperatures or just because they're sadistic evil monsters. We're sick. We need sleep. Got that?

And here is the most important right:

9. Female nurses shall not be unexpectedly present when certain columnists are getting certain medical procedures performed on them involving certain regions of their body for certain baby-preventing purposes. Nor, when said columnist mildly whines about it, shall said female nurse who is present anyway say, "Don't worry, I've seen a million of them, and honey, yours ain't nothing special."

–August 12, 2001

Ten reasons
we need
more power

The typical thing to say after the power goes out is how
much old-time fun you had, and, gee, wouldn't it be
fun if we had more outages?

Let me answer that succintly: No. It wouldn't. We'd
be miserable without our power.

When the lights go out, people light candles and play board
games, then come to work the next day and say how
wonderful it all was.

But I always ask, "If those things are so much fun, how
come you don't do them when the power comes on?"

Because power is more fun. TVs are great. VCRs rule.
Monopoly? Let me tell you something. You know what the
most popular version of Monopoly is right now? A computer
version. Case closed.

I freely admit that I am a slave to electricity. I couldn't do
without it. And I am not alone.

The other day, the entire city of San Francisco was
without power for seven long hours. Trolleys and stoplights
didn't work, snarling traffic. Computers, faxes and elevators
didn't work, paralyzing businesses. Worst of all, the city's 84
trillion coffee shops couldn't make latte.

I know. The horror!

Even more horrific: no water heaters. That meant few
baths and showers. That meant an epidemic of BO. That
means San Francisco was not a pleasant place to be without

a gas mask that day, my friends.

Things fall apart fast without power. Look at Ted Kaczynski, aka the Unabomber. He was a relatively sane guy until he moved into a small cabin in the woods without electricity. Then, boom. (Literally.)

And don't forget what happened in "Jurassic Park" when the electrified fences went cold. The dinosaurs went berserk and ate everyone.

That probably wouldn't happen in real life, but I'm sure other bad things would happen.

I made a list of them, from a personal perspective.

If there were no electricity, there would be no:

1. Television. And if there were no television, there would be no "Baywatch." I shudder just thinking about it.

2. VCR. And if there were no VCR, there would be no Disney tapes to mesmerize the kiddies and if they were no mesmerization, my wife and I would never get 15 minutes peace and we would be forced to offer them up for adoption.

3. Automatic garage door openers. Garage doors don't even operate manually, do they?

4. Coffee makers. Juan Valdez is my Joe Camel. So if you think those people in San Fran were cranky without their morning caffeine, you ain't seen nothin' yet. I am an ugly, ugly person in the morning without coffee. Ask my wife.

5. My home computer. Years ago, I wrote about how no one really needed a home computer. Then I got one and quickly realized how vital they are. I had no idea how empty my life was without instant access to box scores and Pamela Anderson photos.

6. Telephones. And without the telephone, how would I tell the various long distance company reps who call during dinner where they can stick their new calling plans, which is one of my chief forms of entertainment.

7. ATMs. If there were no ATMs, I would have to go back to using living, breathing tellers again. Tellers usually act like I am a MAJOR inconvenience in their day, and that makes me want to kill them, and I don't think I'd like prison food.

8. Microwaves. And if there were no microwaves I would have to eat nothing but cold food the rest of my life. I know there's a device called a "stove" somewhere in our kitchen, but I would need a map to find it.

9. Answering machines. How would I avoid talking to people I don't want to talk to?

10. My office computer, without which I wouldn't be able to write these brilliant ...

– December 14, 1998

These ideas should really fly

Al Gore wants an Air Travelers Bill of Rights. It won't include the following, but it should:

1. Airports shall have enough parking. If the airport runs out of spots, tow trucks shall be called in to haul away the vehicles of airline employees one by one, beginning with management, until such time as every paying passenger has a place to park.

2. Said parking spots shall be in the same telephone area code as the terminal. And if not, the airline will pay for a limousine, complete with a hot tub and several comely attendants of the appropriate gender, to act as a shuttle.

3. The same goes for when I - I mean we - have to change planes and the connecting gate is a Hubble telescope view away.

4. Airfare rates shall make sense, as the author of this Bill of Rights may very well kill someone the next time he sits next to a guy who paid $50 less for a ticket to the same destination.

5. Airline management shall be required to sit in a coach seat until such time as their bodies become one large cramp. This should take several minutes, at most.

6. If, upon realizing that coach seats are too small for actual human beings, airline management fails to rectify the situation via the immediate installation of Barca-loungers, airline management shall be beaten severely about the head with tray tables.

7. Airlines shall be required to install double armrests on all

seats so as to stem the rising tide of vicious mid-air elbow wars among passengers.

8. Flight attendants shall be required to explain why it is necessary to return seats to their upright and locked position when, in the event of a crash, we're all going to be human puree anyway.

9. Airlines shall explain why, no matter how booked a flight is, no matter how many hundreds of people are in line, no matter how much rioting breaks out, they steadfastly refuse to assign more counter people. (Actual reason: "We hate you.")

10. Airlines shall explain why it is necessary to show up an hour and a half before a flight that is subsequently canceled.

11. Flight attendants shall be required to say "I'm SO sorry about this" when dispensing in-flight meals.

12. Airlines shall forgo their current practice of hiring only surly people at the counter and replace said grouches with cast members from "Up With People."

13. Free booze for everybody for the rest of the flight after the first strange mechanical noise.

14. First-class seating shall be in the back of the plane, as we cut-rate passengers find it irritating to have to walk past those snoots relaxing in their huge chairs drinking their white wine while we, the steerage passengers from the Titanic, trip clumsily down the aisle with our carry-ons.

15. Airlines shall allow more carry-on luggage not less until such time as they quit losing the bags we check in, particularly those bags containing our underwear and personal hygiene products.

16. Metal detector operators shall never, ever, while looking at their little screens, say in a loud tone, "Say, Bob, does this look like a tube of hemorrhoid cream to you or a gun?"

17. Flight attendants shall lead formal prayer sessions as the plane rumbles down the runway, since that's what we're all doing anyway.

18. Airlines shall under no circumstance seat a talker next to me.

19. I shall board first. Always.

20. I get to fly the plane whenever I want, too.

– March 15, 1999

Good law, no butts about it

A lawmaker in Maine wants to make cigarette butts returnable. Like bottles. Bring in a butt, get a nickel.

Good idea.

I hate cigarette butts. More specifically, I hate the cigarette smokers who treat the world like their personal ashtray.

You have the butt flicker. You know him. You're driving down the road at night when all of a sudden, a light goes dancing across the pavement. You're startled for a moment until you realize the driver ahead of you has just decided to endanger you (hey, you could swerve, it could happen) and litter.

I caught up to a butt flicker at a light once and said, "Hey, stop littering. You want I should throw fast-food wrappers out the window?"

He blew smoke at me and sped off.

Typical.

Then there's the butt dumper. Butt dumpers are most active at the end of freeway ramps where there is a red light. To you and me, a red light means stop. To a butt dumper, a red light means stop, open car door, deposit contents of ashtray on the ground.

Again, I once honked at a woman in front of me who dumped her butts. She hollered back that if I didn't like her dumping butts, I could kiss hers.

Charming. And typical.

And of course you have the doorway lurkers. Every
business has them. They're the ones who stand outside in all
kinds of weather huddled over their smoking sticks of tobacco.

I've always felt a bit sorry for doorway lurkers. They're
pariahs. No business will let them smoke inside anymore, so
they're forced into doorways and alleys and behind
Dumpsters.

I feel a lot less sorry when I see the mess they make. Even
when they're given ashtrays to use, they can't manage to get
their butts into them. Either years of exposure to smoke has
limited their vision or like many smokers, they just don't care.
You know which it is.

(Note to smokers: OK, if you're not just being littering pigs,
then tell me: Where do you suppose your butt goes when you
throw it or flick it or toss it out a window? Into some
alternative universe filled with fairies who pick it up for you?
Sorry, it's not true. Those fairies are busy picking my
underwear up off the floor at home.)

Smokers, naturally, are upset about the butt bill, which
was introduced by state Rep. Joe Brooks. They cry about how
it would add another dollar to the cost of a pack.

I'm not feeling too much sympathy here. How about the
cost to society in terms of uglying up the environment?

Another buck won't kill you. Maybe the nickel you'd get
back for every butt would be enough to persuade you that the
rest of us shouldn't have to suffer because of your dumb
habit. (And I mean in addition to all the other ways we suffer
because of your habit: stinking clothes, ruined meals,
cancerous lungs, etc.)

Not to worry, though. Even if you butt-dumpers don't start
picking up after yourselves, I guarantee there will be no
shortage of people who will. People always pick up bottles and
cans in states where they are returnable.

Personally, if this butt bill spreads across the country, I'm
planning to keep a garbage bag and a large coal shovel in my
car.

Betcha I can send the kiddies to college on the freeway
ramps alone.

Jet boats ruin our solitude

– March 18, 2000

I was sitting on the shore of Lake Michigan, peacefully swatting at mosquitos and waiting for the sun to set, when they came, as I knew that they would.

Nnnnnnnynaaaaaaaaaaaar!

Rrrrrrrrrrrowwwwwww!

Sssssssssshwoooof!

I muttered angrily under my breath the way Seinfeld mutters at Newman, except I muttered, "Jet Skis!"

Lord, I hate Jet Skis. And Wave Runners. And any other loud, obnoxious jet-powered boat that qualifies as a "personal watercraft."

If I had my way, each and every one of them would be melted down and used for a more useful purpose, such as filling potholes.

Better yet, melt down the people who operate them like selfish idiots and use THEM to fill the potholes.

The only problem with that idea, however, is that Jet Ski owners tend to be young, flabless types, so it would take a lot of them to fill even one pothole. Not to worry. I doubt we'll run out. Jet boats, along with cell phones, leaf blowers and Celine Dion, seem to be a modern evil that isn't going away any time soon.

They are everywhere. On every lake. On every river. On

every body of water larger than my bathtub.

In fact, the other day, I was in my bathtub, up to my neck in Mr. Bubble, when - vroooom! - a personal watercraft came sweeping by and sprayed me. I nearly drowned!

OK, it was my 4-year-old with a plastic motorboat. He dropped it in the tub, went "Nyarrr! Nyarrr!" splashed me, and ran away laughing.

But the point's the same: jet boats are bugging me.

One of my favorite things to do in the whole world is to sit on the shore of a lake - any lake, anywhere - and stare.

It's better if I'm alone, or if the lake is unmarred by humans. But I'm not a purist. I take what I can get. A busy beach with with my kids running around and slopping Popsicle juice on me is OK, too.

It's still nice. You get a feeling from staring at lakes that you don't get from staring at anything else. Even Cameron Diaz. And jet boats ruin that. They're just too damned noisy. Haven't the people who make them ever heard of Tuffy Muffler?

I read a news story the other day in which a manufacturer swore the industry had made great strides in making jet boats quieter. I had to laugh. They don't in truth want to make jet boats quiet any more than Harley-Davidson wants to make motorcycles that go "putt-putt-putt" instead of "Grrrrumble-ROOOAR!" To jet boat owners, the noise is half the fun. Riding a jet boat that didn't make noise would be like watching TV with the sound off.

The problem, of course, is that sound carries exceptionally well over water. So one jet boat can disturb peace-craving ninnies like me for a mile in any direction.

Each year, I rent a cabin on a lake so breathtaking that National Geographic magazine once called it one of the most beautiful in the world. The world! And, yet, the last time I was there, never once between the hours of 9 a.m., when the jet skiers arose from their Mountain Dew slumbers, and 10 p.m., when the sun set, was the lake free of the mosquito-buzz of jet boats. I haven't gone back since. There's no point. I can't stare in the dark.

Am I the only one these days who thinks that's a bad thing? That maybe we're losing something? Judging from the hate mail I'm about to receive, I would say yes.

But I don't care. All I know is that God help us if Boeing or Lockheed ever develops an air-borne equivalent. You won't be safe in your own back yard. You'll yell, "Honey, get the can of Raid. We got Air-Skis again!"

And earplugs will be worn by all.

– July 19, 1998

The little annoyances are the most annoying

Big problems do not bother me. Death. Taxes. Running out of beer at halftime.

It is the little things that I can't handle. They bother me beyond all reason. I do not know why.

I will give you two examples: compact discs and shoelaces. First, the compact discs.

I have a small life, so buying a compact disc is still a big thing to me. I get excited. I can't wait to get home and open the little box and play the music.

But I can't. You cannot get into those things.

First, you have to get past the first line of defense - the shrink wrap. Shrink wrap is tough stuff. Forget the Star Wars defense program. Build a dome over the country made of shrink wrap. No missile will ever get through.

I have particular trouble with shrink wrap because I have no fingernails.

Well, not NO fingernails. That would be kind of bizarre. But short ones. I drink too much coffee, so I bite them.

So I have to find a knife to cut the stuff off. Then I get excited again because now I can open the box and take out the shiny CD and play that funky music, white boy.

Wait. No I can't. There's that teeny-tiny piece of tape they put along the top edge for no apparent reason.

I hate that tape.

There is a little tab that you pull to strip the tape off clean.

But that tab is like the little string in the little paper package around a Band-Aid. It doesn't work. Maybe in the lab it works. Maybe it works when they're showing it off to compact disc executives. But in real life it is as useless as Tom Arnold's appendix. (What do you mean you don't get that? Tom Arnold is useless. So what would be more useless than a useless actor's most useless organ? See, I'm a funny guy. You just don't know it.)

Eventually, I have to use the knife again. I carve and slice and peel with it until finally I get that stupid tape off.

By then I'm so mad I need the music to calm down.

The typical result is I pledge never again to buy a compact disc, at least until I forget about the tape and the shrink wrap.

Then there are shoelaces.

I play a lot of sports, so I buy a lot of tennis shoes. (There's another small thing that bugs me. Relatively few people play tennis in their tennis shoes, so why are they called tennis shoes?) (And, no, I won't call them sneakers, either. I do even less sneaking in them than tennis playing.)

Every single pair I have purchased in the past five years has come with shoelaces that are at least a foot too long.

No. I am not exaggerating. When I lace them up, I usually have about an extra 6 inches of lace at each end.

I do not know what to do with it. I make enormous bunny ears, loops so big, in fact, that you could snare actual rabbits with them, but that only takes up a few inches. I also double-knot. But that's only another inch. So what am I to do?

I've tried cutting them to the appropriate length. But then the ends unravel, and I can never get them back through the eyelets if they slip out.

Someone once said to me, "Why don't you dip the ends in paraffin?"

What, I'm Martha Stewart now?

What I want to know is why shoe manufacturers do this to me? There's got to be a reason. They must KNOW they're too long, right?

The only two possible explanations: 1) They somehow think the idea of an entire nation of mopes like me tripping over big bunny ears is funny, or 2) Somehow it's considered fashionable.

Either way, it makes me irrationally angry.
I'm not buying any more compact discs.
Maybe I'll stop buying shoes, too.
That'll fix 'em.

–November 9, 1998

James Bond stuff we need on the road

A friend who knows my disdain for the driving habits of everybody who isn't me asked, "Did you see the story a few weeks ago about the guy in South Africa who invented a car door flame thrower to incinerate would-be car-jackers?"

I did indeed.

"Well, what'd you think?"

I think they must have lots of car-jackers in South Africa.

"And?"

And if drivers flambe a few dozen of them, they won't have a lot of them very much longer. So I think it's a good idea.

"That's it? Just a good idea? Those are your entire thoughts on the matter?"

Well, no. I also wonder what they use to get fried car-jacker off the door panels. You seem disappointed.

"It's just that I thought you'd be thrilled. Aren't you the one who's always saying you're the world's only good driver?"

Yes, I do say that. And I am. So?

"So I thought you might want to order one or something."

I would if we had a car-jacker problem in this country, but we don't, so why bother? I can think of things that would be far more useful than a flame thrower.

"Now we're getting somewhere. Give me details."

Well, for one thing, I think cars should come equipped with oil slick-makers.

"Oil slicks?"

Sure. Just like the James Bond movies. I hate being tailgated. One oil slick and, fwoop, no more tailgater.

"Go on."

I also think we could use a nose-picking device on air bags.

"I don't follow."

Simple. There's nothing more nauseating than being stopped at a light next to a guy who is knuckle deep in the nostril caves, right?

"Right."

So someone should invent a sensor on the steering wheel that activates the air bag once finger insertion is detected.

"I don't follow."

The bag rams the guy's finger so far up there, he'll end up picking his cerebral cortex.

"Wow, that's savage."

It's a savage world. I also think cars should come with those pronged hydraulic lifts they have on the front of garbage trucks to lift Dumpsters.

"What for?"

For parking lots. You know how there's always some idiot who can't figure out how to park between the lines? Or, worse, there's that driver with the really swanky car who parks diagonal across two spots so no one scratches his precious paint job?

"Yeah."

Well, you spike his car with your prongs, lift it and find a convenient dumping ground, preferably in a nearby river. If the driver is in it at the time, so much the better.

"So how would you solve the problem of slow drivers in the fast lane?"

Simple. Land mines.

"Land mines?"

Yup. Equip the fast lane of all freeways with a series of land mines that any driver can activate by pushing a button on his dashboard. If someone is driving slow in the fast lane, they get 10 seconds to move over or ka-blam.

"Anything else?"

Jerk boards.

"Jerk boards?"

You know those lighted message boards where the words

crawl across? I want one of those on the back of my car to communicate with drivers behind me. The keyboard to program it would be right next to my seat. It would have reinforced A and F keys, since I would be using words that begin with those letters quite a bit.

"Sheesh, that's pretty brutal. Remind me never to tick you off in traffic."

Hey, Bill.

"What?"

Never tick me off in traffic.

– February 22, 1999

Personally, I need a spokesperson

Perhaps it's the heat, but I think I have a good idea here. I got this idea while reading an article about Hugh Grant and his girlfriend, model Elizabeth Hurley.

Grant, in case you've been absent from the planet recently, is the actor who was arrested for failing to have enough cash on him to rent a hotel room, if you catch my drift.

Anyway, this article contained the following paragraph: "Meanwhile, Hurley's camp also denies reports of a breakup (with Grant). 'They have not officially decided to split,' spokeswoman Karin Smith said Monday."

I read that and my immediate reaction was "What a ridiculous way to spell Karen." My second immediate reaction was, "Elizabeth Hurley has a camp! Even better, she's got a spokesperson!"

This is a woman few people outside the fashion world had heard about before her boyfriend's tragic lack of pocket change. And yet she's got a "camp" and a "spokesperson."

That's amazing. Used to be only truly important people had spokespersons. Presidents. Rich guys. Gangsters.

Now models have them.

And if models can have them, well, here's my idea: spokespersons for the common man and woman.

You like?

Listen, it's not so far-fetched. Nannies, maids and lawn services used to be for the upper crust. Now many of my friends have them. And trust me, my friends are not upper crust. They are more like day-old crust. And if they can have nannies, maids and lawn services, why not spokespersons?

Think of the uses. No longer would you have to confront embarrassing or troublesome situations in your life. You simply have your spokesperson release "statements" on your behalf.

I'll use myself to illustrate.

Say my boss is furious with me for making $6,000 worth of calls to 1-900-555-MOAN on the company dime. (Not, ha-ha, that I've ever done anything like that!) (Recently, I mean.)

Instead of stammering through a long-winded but ultimately see-through excuse about how I merely misdialed the cable company rates recording over and over and over again, I have my spokesperson say: "Mr. Heller has informed me that he steadfastly maintains his innocence in this matter. He regards the charges as, quote, 'slanderous, libelous and really, really mean' and is currently consulting with an attorney about possible legal action."

Or say my wife storms into the den to accuse me of yet again leaving a used apple core, a dirty plate and an empty beer bottle on the living room floor.

Instead of abjectly apologizing and promising for the millionth time to never, ever do it again, I wave my hand and my spokesperson intercedes.

"I'm sorry," my spokesperson will politely but firmly inform my wife, "but Mr. Heller is not available for comment today."

Parents could hire spokespersons for their kids.

"I'm sorry, Mrs. Applebee, but Little Timmy will have no further comment at this time about the tragic consumption of his homework assignment by his dog, Ralph."

Motorists could have a spokesperson in the car with them in case they are pulled over: "Officer, my client has authorized me to shamelessly suck-up to you, up to and including offering you his box seats for tomorrow's baseball game, in order to convince you to let him out of this ticket."

The possibilities are endless, which is why I firmly believe that this is an idea whose time has come.

Or, like I said, it could be the heat.

—July 17, 1995

Hunting
in the
Twilight Zone

I *f deer ran the world ...*

"Hi Buck, howya doing?"

"Just fine, Spike. And you?"

"Other than a few ticks and a touch of tuberculosis, I can't complain. Say, how's that wife of yours?"

"She's fine, but you know does. Always complaining about something."

"Ain't it the truth. Say, you going hunting this year? It's almost time, you know."

"Wouldn't miss it. I hear the city's positively overrun with people this year."

"Tell me about it. I nearly hit another one of them again the other day. The thing about people is they're so darned stupid. There I'll be, standing in the road, minding my own business, when, vroom, here comes one of 'em barreling at me in a car. And they don't look. They never look. And when they finally do see you they just stare at you with that weird frozen look."

"I know, like a human in a headlight."

"The problem is there's just too many of them."

"I know, I know. I personally feel a deep and abiding responsibility to cull the herd. That's the only reason I go hunting year after year."

"Oh, come on, you don't get the teensiest thrill when you run one of 'em through with your antlers?"

"No, no. I'm a conservationist. It's all about harvesting and good herd management. You know that."

"I know, I know. I'm just messing with you. If the human population gets out of control we all know what'll happen."

"Rampant suburbanization?"

"You got it. Plus you-know-what else."

"Strip malls?"

"Yup. Plus, really, with a lot of 'em, we're doing 'em a favor."

"Darned right. There's so many, a lot of them will starve during the winter."

"I know. The poor creatures. That's why I go out and gore one each year, whether I'm in the mood or not."

"Say, you gonna bait again this year?"

"Oh, absolutely. I don't have time to stalk humans. I gotta get in, get out. I'm thinking of using fried cheese balls this year. I hear humans go for 'em like candy."

"Not me. I'm going with the old tried and true."

"French fries?"

"Yup. They go nuts for them. Especially the young males. I think they like the salt. They must not get enough in their regular diet. Anyway, I've never, ever failed to fill my license using french fries."

"How you gonna get your human home this year?"

"Same way as always. Strap it on my back."

"Ooo, my wife hates that. Says she can't stand seeing 'em with their tongues hanging out and their eyes all googly."

"Yeah, my wife, too. She's one of those wacko human rights activists. But what do they want us to do? We gotta get 'em home to the human pole somehow."

"Dang right. The human pole is the highlight of the year!"

"You know it. I positively burst with pride when we hang 'em all up there in the town square with their guts ripped open, and the rest of the herd gathers around to admire the big ones."

"That is a special moment."

"You bet. But you know what my fruity younger brother Bambi said? He said we shouldn't hang 'em up like that because it's disrespectful."

"Hey, we gotta let the blood drain out somehow. Sheesh, what a wimp. How can you disrespect a dumb animal anyhow?"

"I don't know. He's got some pretty weird ideas."

– November 24, 1999

Ads give me a shill - er, thrill

I have another great idea.

Allow me to share.

The other day I was reading along in the newspaper - read, read, read - when I came across a story buried deep inside headlined "Drivers lease bumper space for ad dollars."

Being a person of much crankiness and little money, I immediately thought, "Great idea."

Apparently, several companies in California, the land of fruits and nuts, are paying drivers to wrap their cars in ads, a la cars on the NASCAR and Indy circuits.

One woman made enough money to pay her monthly car loan, so basically she was driving for free. The only cost: a few stares.

But so what? Stares aren't any worse than fingers, which is what most of us are used to getting on the road. And you have to admit, you'd never have trouble finding your car in the mall parking lot if it were painted McDonald's yellow and had a picture of the Hamburglar on the side.

The article quoted a professor at a New York university who sniffed that the idea was crass and creepy.

"What's next - to pay people to have ads tattooed on their foreheads?" he said.

Probably. But what's wrong with that? I know some people who would look quite smashing with a Pennzoil logo on their noggins.

I'd sell my forehead. I'd also sell space on my car.

Perhaps, in your mind, that makes me a shill.

Maybe. But don't be so quick to judge. Most Americans have been walking billboards for one company or another for years.

Check your closet. See any T-shirts with the Nike swoosh in there? How about a shirt with your favorite tavern's name on it? How about your tennis shoes? See the manufacturers name in big bold letters?

Then you're already helping them out.

Or how about your car? You might think the idea of your car being nothing more than a rolling commercial is repellent. But I'll bet you any money that your car not only prominently features the manufacturer's name but the dealership's name as well.

If so, a rolling advertisement is exactly what you are.

Many people, in fact, become living, breathing advertisements on purpose. They'll spend extra money to buy clothing that prominently features the maker's name. I see people all the time wearing shirts emblazoned with Abercrombie & Fitch or Old Navy or the University of Michigan.

Now, clearly those people are status seekers. They think that by showing off their good taste in clothes or universities or whatever that people will think, "Oh, gosh, isn't he swell!"

But really, it shows what dupes for corporate America they are. I'm a dupe. You're a dupe. We might as well benefit from it.

Thus, I would like to take this opportunity to say to the companies of America that I am up for sale. Here I am. Come get me. Have a headache pill you want to hustle? My forehead goes for a mere $100 per week. Got some jeans you want to push? My butt's available for $50 per cheek. (Don't scoff. That'll buy you lots of square footage.)

I'll rent out space on my car, my house, my kids. Anything, anywhere. For a price. Make me an offer.

That may make me a shill.

But I'll be a shill who gets paid for what most of us do for free.

– July 31, 2000

How to flush out dishonest researchers

A recent news story has led me to the belief that we need extremely stiff penalties for scientists and researchers who scare the public without knowing what they're talking about.

The story concerned toilets. A few years ago, a University of Arizona scientist named Charles Gerba published a study that said when you flush the toilet little bits of fecal material fly into the air and get all over everything. Including nearby toothbrushes.

I remember reading about this study. It scared me to death, as I am highly and regrettably susceptible to believing things I read in print, no matter how bizarre.

So I ended up worrying, "Toilet water? Fecal material? Good grief, I might as well brush my teeth with the toilet scrubber." Sure, toilet water never seems to do dogs any harm, but then I had a dog once whose favorite restaurant was Chez Litter Box.

I worried so much about this study that I kept my toothbrush in a drawer thereafter. And even then a small part of me was unnerved. I would look at my toothbrush in the morning and wonder what other microscopic creepy crawlies were on there. Brushing was never the same after that.

Now, of course, I learn that I had nothing to fear. Another study now says the earlier study is full of fecal material. It said toilet germs don't go airborne, as previously thought. They go down the drain. End of story.

So once again we've been duped. This happens too often these days. Some scientist who wants to see his name in print studies something that no one ever thought to worry about before, discovers something horrifying and writes a paper on it for some medical journal, which is then picked up by the media, especially during sweeps week.

And before you know it, we're all fretting about Chinese food. Or Mexican food. Or wine (now considered beneficial; I'll drink to that.) Or airbags (said to have injured a few small children; forget how many they've saved). Or global warming. (It was hard to concentrate on this frightening prospect this past winter and spring, what with all the snow.)

Or, worse, we're gulping down dreadful junk like oat bran because some near-sighted test-tube sniffer says it will suck cholesterol out of our systems faster than Dom DeLuise sucks the filling out of cannoli.

Then, a year later, you can count on another study contradicting the first, which is the scientific equivalent of saying, "Whoops."

And what happens to the moron who was proven wrong?

Nothing. He already got his publicity and the resulting research grant. He's happier than a pig in the aforementioned toilet material. He couldn't care less that he caused millions of people needless worry.

That, my friends, is not right. There oughta be a law. You can't yell "fire!" in a public building if there isn't a fire. Nor should you be able to say, "Watch out, toilet cooties!"

I propose the following. I say any researcher who ballyhoos a scary study that later turns out to be false be tried and found guilty of first degree worry inducement.

A fitting punishment might be having a hypnotist implant frightening but erroneous beliefs into the the accused's brain for the same length of time that he or she made the public worry.

These beliefs could be something such as tap water causes cancer or blinking causes blindness.

Or in Mr. Gerba's case, we could implant the thought that toilet seats have teeth. He'd never go in peace again.

How fitting indeed.

– June 2, 1996

A victory against the PC police

Finally, a victory for our side. Our side, in this case, being the victims of the P.C. Police.

P.C. stands for Political Correctness. (Although it could just as easily stand for Persnickety Crackpots or Purposely Crotchety.)

It's been a wonderful decade so far for the P.C. Police.

They've turned manholes into maintenance access portals, women into womyn, every possible ethnic or racial group into hyphen-Americans and short into vertically challenged.

They have changed the way we speak and live.

Tell a co-worker he or she looks nice today and you risk a sexual harassment complaint.

Tell a joke involving anybody other than a white male (for some reason we're still fair game) and they'll haul you off to a re-education gulag.

Call a woman "sweetheart" if she is not in fact your sweetheart and you risk a lawsuit and/or a groin injury.

Say that Pat Buchanan might just have one or two good ideas and they'll call you a Nazi (or, rather, a morally deficit person of Germanic ancestry).

It's a different world.

But now maybe the tide is turning. The P.C. Police finally lost one. And the best thing is, it's all because of a black woman - sorry, an African-American person of the female persuasion.

Her name is Bernice Harris. I read about her in the papers.

Ms. Harris has been a cashier for a coffee shop inside the U.S. Senate in Washington, D.C., for 30 years.

And in all that time she had never had a problem with anybody.

Then, a few weeks ago, out of the blue, she received a sexual harassment complaint. No, she didn't pinch Strom Thurmond's rear end or tell Bob Dole to smile once in a while, for crying out loud.

What happened is she called a Senate staffer "baby," as in "How you doing today, baby?" and he took offense.

Harris was upset about the charge because she calls everyone baby, honey or sweetheart, from deliverypersons to the senators themselves.

So when her supervisors decided to transfer her rather than risk a lawsuit from the upset staffer, she quit.

Now this is the part that does my heart good.

After Harris quit, Senate staffers and even a few senators rallied to her side. It seems they actually liked being called baby or sweet-cheeks or honey pie when they purchased gum or newspapers from Harris.

So she got her job back. And she can still call her customers (except for Mr. Sensitive) whatever she likes.

I find this particularly heartening because I come from a long line of people who use terms of endearment.

My Grandma Rose, God rest her sweet Southern soul, called many people, but particularly her six grandkids, "sugar," although with her Carolina accent it came out "shugah." Rest assured, if Rose called you "shugah" it meant you were all right with her.

My other grandmother, the refined Jean, calls people "dear." And my mother still calls me "sweetie."

The practice carried over to me. I used to call female friends and acquaintances "sweetie" or "babe." To me it meant I liked and was comfortable with them. But as times changed, I changed. And these days, for fear of being misunderstood, I restrict my "sweeties" and "babes" to just my closest female chums.

But maybe now I'll haul them out and brush them off, especially if the backlash against the P.C. Police continues.

That all right with you, shugah?

April 1, 1996

Pricey food dims the theater experience

I went to the movies recently.

That's a switch. I all but stopped going to the movies five years ago after my first child was born. I'm a frugal consumer - my wife calls it cheap, but that's semantics - and the only thing more expensive than a movie out is a babysitter in.

Put one on top of the other, you've got yourself an expensive night, and all to watch Arnold Schwarzenegger blow things up. No thanks.

So some things about the movies are new to me.

Such as the cost of popcorn.

"I'll take the largest popcorn you have," I said to the counter girl, who had that look of irritated boredom that all clerks have.

"That's $4.75," she grunted.

"Four seventy five?" I said. "No, no, dear. You don't understand. I already have my movie ticket. I wanted popcorn. You know, popcorn. Yum, yum. White, fluffy stuff? It's right there." (Yes, I know I shouldn't use sarcasm with clerks, but I can't help it. I'm a bad person.)

"That's the price of the popcorn," she said. "So you want it or not?"

I had three kids in tow, so I said yes. But $4.75 for popcorn is, I'm sorry, highway robbery. No wait, it's worse than that. It's come-into-your-home-and-rob-you-in-front-of-your-family robbery. For $4.75, you ought to get a giganto bucket of corn - a bucket big enough to haul trash in. Instead, you get ... a bag. A bag! And it's a bag about the size of a lunch sack.

"Um, excuse me," I said. "I ordered the large."

"That is the large," she said. "Anything else?"

"Uh, drinks," I said. "Gimme four pops, but make 'em smalls."

"That'll be $10."

Oh, for crying out loud. Two-fifty per pop and $4.75 for popcorn? That's ridiculous. I grumbled all the way through the movie. Then, when I got home, I grumbled to my wife, who loves it when I go off on a rant about modern life.

"Can you change the baby, please?" she said, hiding her passionate agreement with my position.

Anyway, I'm a bit of a crank when it comes to these things, so I went back to the theater a few days later and bought another popcorn and a pop. Total cost: $7.25. Then I went home and measured what I was getting.

"Oh, for ..." my wife said when she walked in the kitchen. "Not again."

"Hand me that measuring cup, wouldya?" I said.

So here's what I got for $7.25: 19 cups of popcorn and 16 ounces of pop.

Then I went to the store. I bought a 1-pound bag of Cousin Willie's unpopped popcorn for 79 cents and a six-pack of pop for $2.99. Each can of pop held 12 ounces, so, let's see, six times 12 is ... 72. So I had 72 ounces of pop for 49 cents more than I paid for a mere 16 ounces at the movies. The back of the Cousin Willie's bag said it contained 13 servings and each serving was four cups popped, so that's ... 52 cups. For those 52 cups, I paid 79 cents. At the theater, 19 cups cost me $4.75.

Can you say "Holy huge ripoff, Batman!"?

I reported these amazing findings to my wife and she rolled her eyes and said, "Can you change the baby, please? He's wet again."

So she shares my outrage.

Now you might be thinking, well, theaters have to make their money some way. They've got labor costs, cooking oil costs, etc. And of course when you go to a theater, you're paying for the experience, the ambience.

But you know what I think?

I think the cost of theater food is why God made VCRs.

–December 1, 1999

Wedded
Bliss

Drowning in marital happiness

O nce again it's time for "Ask Dr. Marriage," the irresponsibly popular advice column for men of the male persuasion who are mystified by the creatures who steal 80 percent of the closet space.

Today's question comes from a close personal friend of Dr. Marriage named Mike McDermott, who, for reasons of anonymity, we will hereafter refer to as "Mike."

Mike writes: "Dear Dr. Marriage: My wife couldn't get enough of me before we had children. She would kiss me warmly when we met at home after work. She would cook me special dinners. We'd nuzzle on the couch. We were blissfully happy. But now that we have three kids, it's like I hardly exist. What happened?"

Mike, Mike, Mike. You fool. You dear, sweet fool. You may feel that you are the only one in the world having this problem but in fact it's quite a common marriage problem.

We therapists call it "Invisible Man Syndrome." The sad, simple truth is that once a woman has children, they come first. And second. And third. You, in essence, have been demoted. After the arrival of kids, the typical male's official household rank falls to somewhere below the toaster.

Don't take this personally. That's just how it is. The important thing is that you understand that you are not alone. Millions of men are in the same boat.

Why, even Dr. Marriage experienced "Invisible Man

Syndrome" recently. The other day, he was discussing the movie "Cast Away" with his wife, Mrs. Dr. Marriage, when the discussion took a mutant turn, as discussions involving Dr. Marriage and his wife often do.

The question was: If Dr. Marriage, his wife and three children were on a sinking ship and there were only four lifejackets, who would get them?

Dr. Marriage thought for a moment, considered the various ethical dilemmas, made the requisite joke about how he should clearly get one because he could always make more children, which elicited a not unexpected and surprisingly painful slug on the arm from Mrs. Dr. Marriage. And then he nobly said, as any right thinking father would, "Why of course you and the kids would get them, sweetheart. But how about you? Who do you think should get them?"

She immediately said, "Me and the kids."

It wasn't the answer itself that surprised Dr. Marriage. It was the speed of the decision. Dr. Marriage timed it at 1.5 nanoseconds.

"Wait a second," Dr. Marriage said. "You're not even going to consider this for a moment?"

"Nope," she said. "The kids would get them because they're kids. And I'd get the last one because the kids need me."

"Oh, so you're saying that they don't need ME?" a wounded Dr. Marriage said.

"Well, duh," she replied. "Who cooks for them? Me. Who cleans for them? Me. Who stays up all night when they have the flu? Me. Are you suddenly going to do all that? Are you? Because if you are, by all means, mister, take the lifejacket. At least I'd get some rest while the boat sinks."

OK, so clearly Dr. Marriage is going to drown.

The point here, Mike, is that you are not alone. Invisible Man Syndrome is a common, common thing. Dr. Marriage doesn't know what, if anything, you can do about it. Some things are beyond even him.

But Dr. Marriage does know this: He's sure as heck never getting on a boat with Mrs. Dr. Marriage.

–April 1, 2001

When in doubt, fake a heart attack

Once again, we bring you "Ask Dr. Marriage," the phenomenally popular column in which we offer advice - usually ridiculously inaccurate - to husbands mystified by the creatures with whom they share influenza germs.

Today's question comes from a close personal friend of Dr. Marriage's named Bob, who, for security reasons, we will call "Bill."

Bill writes: "Dear Dr. Marriage: Recently, my wife asked me if I remembered our first kiss and I said no because, you know, I didn't, and now she's mad at me. I don't think I should be expected to remember something that happened 20 years ago. What do you think?"

Dr. Marriage thinks Bill is an idiot, that's what Dr. Marriage thinks.

Of COURSE he should have remembered. And if he didn't remember, he should have distracted her somehow, perhaps by faking a heart attack.

Because women not only expect you to remember the key moments of your courtship - your first kiss, including where you were, what she was wearing and what the meteorological conditions were at the time, the first time you fought, and of course the first time you insulted her mother - they will KILL you if you don't.

Dr. Marriage had a similar experience recently.

He walked into the family room to get the newspaper and said idly to his wife, who was watching TV, "Whatcha watching, honey?"

This was Dr. Marriage's second mistake. (The first was being born.)

His wife said, "It's a news magazine report about that guy who advertised in the paper for a bride."

"He advertised for a wife?" said Dr. Marriage.

"Yes, and this woman replied and they got married, all without so much as one date."

"Really?" said Dr. Marriage.

"Really. And now they're checking back with them three months into their marriage to see how things are going."

Dr. Marriage sat and watched for awhile. This was his third mistake. The couple, it seems, was getting along fine. But at one point, the interviewer asked the man if he even knew what color his wife's eyes were. He stammered and said, "Blue?" They were brown.

The interviewer then asked other questions about what he knew about her, including what her shoe size is. He got every one wrong.

"At least he's got an excuse," Dr. Marriage's wife snorted. "He's only known her for three months. You've know me for 20 years and you don't know anything about me."

At this point, sensing danger, Dr. Marriage attempted to scuttle from the room like a frightened lobster. But she said, "Get back here, you coward. I want to test you."

"Don't be ridiculous," Dr. Marriage said. "I know plenty about you."

"Oh, really? So what's my favorite color?"

"Blue?" said Dr. Marriage.

"Wrong," said Mrs. Dr. Marriage.

"I know, red!"

"Wrong. It's purple. So what's my favorite TV show?"

" 'Friends'?"

"Wrong. 'Spin City.' What's my favorite book."

"Um, 'The Color Purple.' (He said this because of the earlier purple association. See how clever Dr. Marriage is?)

"Wrong. It's 'The Prince of Tides.' What's my shoe size?"

"Uh, 10?"

"Eight. What am I, a lumberjack? You really don't know

anything at all about me, do you? You really don't know the..."

Dr. Marriage would tell you how this conversation ended, but oddly enough that is when he suffered a fatal heart attack.

– November 23, 1998

Guys just don't get self-help books

You do that," said the lovely yet formidable Marcia.

We were in bed. She was on her side watching TV. I was on my side trying to pretend I was asleep.

"You do that, too," she said, nudging me.

Another minute passed.

"Wow, and that, too!" Nudge, nudge. "I know you're faking. Now roll over and watch this with me. You might learn something."

Cripes, I hate self-help books.

That's what she was watching: a news magazine show about a self-help book, specifically "Men Are From Mars, Women Are From the Planet of My Husband Leaves His Underpants on the Floor and Expects *ME* To Pick Up After Him." Or something like that.

Marcia, like most women, is big into self-help books, particularly this one (which, all right, is actually called "Men Are From Mars, Women Are From the Land of My Bonehead Husband Forgot Our Anniversary").

Women love these books because they are constantly trying to improve themselves and their relationships with men, other women, children, small mammals including ferrets, buildings, ficus plants and small, undeveloped nations.

Women, relationship-wise, basically want to buy the world a Coke and sing in harmony. Whereas men are far more likely to buy the world a Coke in order to have a belching contest.

And not because we don't care about our relationships with other people. We do. Just in different ways.

By that I mean men tend to deal with relationships the way we deal with broken household appliances: leave them alone long enough and eventually they'll fix themselves, or whatever, while we watch a ballgame.

But back to the news show. The basic premise was this: John Gray, who wrote the book "Men Are From Mars, Women Frequently Wish They'd Stay There," was interviewing couples on stage in front of an audience about what was wrong in their relationships.

The typical female response: "Well, for starters, he doesn't help with the kids, doesn't cook, doesn't clean, stays late at the office, couldn't locate our washing machine with a compass, leaves piles of newspapers and toenail clippings on the floor, watches sports on TV incessantly, and then he wants sex all the time. Plus he snores."

The typical male response: "Hey, I don't snore!"

Then the women in the audience would groan, while the men next to them looked sheepish. Then women all over America would elbow their husbands and say, "See, you do that." Then Gray, author of the book "Men Are From Mars, I'm Making Kazillions of Dollars," would scold the men on stage and tell them to be more "empathetic."

You could see most of the guys had no idea what that meant. Many of them were probably thinking it had something to do with putting the toilet seat down.

But, OK, they all said, they'd try it, especially if it meant they got more sex.

Then the women in the audience would groan again. And finally the women at home would elbow their husbands again as if THEY had said it, when really all we were trying to do is pretend we were asleep so we didn't have to hear about our numerous shortcomings.

I didn't much like this show. But at least I got a good idea out of it.

I've decided to write my own book. I'll call it "Women Are From Mars, Self-Help Authors Ought to be Stripped Naked, Dipped in Caramel, Rolled in McDonald's French Fries, Then Strapped to a Picnic Table at a Public Beach With a Million Starving Seagulls." I'm sure it'll be a best-seller.

Ask any guy.

–September 14, 1997

It must be the dust ... or the work

Men, you'll be happy to know that once again I have defended our honor. And with stunning brilliance, if I may be so bold.

I was using the copy machine here at work and began chatting with the secretary who works nearby.

She was annoyed at her husband, who had recently failed to complete some household chore she had assigned to him.

"You're a man," she said. "So tell me, what is it with your gender?"

"What do you mean?" I asked.

"How come you're so allergic to cleaning?"

"That's it exactly," I said. "You've hit the nail on the head."

"Huh?"

"We're allergic to cleaning."

"You mean physically allergic? That's absurd."

"Au contraire," I said. (Women love it when you speak French to them.) "There's a growing body of scientific evidence indicating that the male of the species is in fact allergic to general housekeeping and that's why he doesn't perform much of it."

"Uh-huh," she said, curling the corner of her mouth. "And was the scientist who came up with that theory a man or a woman?"

"A man," I said. "But that has nothing to do with the findings. We're talking scientific fact here."

"That's the most ridiculous thing I've ever heard."

"It's not ridiculous at all," I said. "There are actual, physical symptoms. You can look it up."

"And these would be?"

"Well," I said, "for starters, when a man is exposed to too much housework he-"

"Wait a second. Too much? How much is too much?"

"More than two minutes," I said. "May I continue?"

"By all means. This is fascinating."

"When a man is exposed to too much housework, he begins to experience an unquenchable thirst."

"Ah, that would explain the beer."

"Exactly. Hops-based hydration is very important in battling this condition."

"I see. Any other `symptoms' "?

"Well, this thirst is followed by a marked trembling of the hands that makes it almost impossible to operate a vacuum cleaner."

"And yet, amazingly enough, it doesn't seem to affect your use of the remote control."

"Exactly!" I cried. "It is indeed a mysterious condition. But the trembling, as bad as it is, is not even the worst of it."

"Do tell."

"No, the worst symptom is an insatiable desire to lie down on the couch and take a nap. The other day, for instance, my wife asked me to clean the bathroom and I immediately felt like Rip van Winkle. I had no choice but to seek out the couch."

"But of course you didn't. Poor baby."

"So you see, it's not really our fault that we don't clean. It's a genetic condition that men are born with, damn the luck. We can no more resist our biological destiny than women can resist their biologically based urge to shop half-off sales."

She rolled her eyes.

"So what you're saying is that women should do all the cleaning and men should do none of it."

"I'm saying nothing of the sort," I snorted. "I'm saying the bulk of the cleaning chores should be left to the experts."

"The experts?"

"You know, the cleaning fairies."

She rolled her eyes again and said she had work to do.

What? She's never heard of cleaning fairies? There's a growing body of scientific evidence indicating that they do, in fact, exist. Honest.

You can look it up.

–March 24, 1997

To men, the clicker is a magic wand

When I am in my black leather La-Z-Boy clicking through the channels, oblivious to the world outside the glowing screen, my wife will sometimes say to me, "I swear you're in love with that thing."

She is not talking about the TV. I am an indifferent TV watcher. I think most sitcoms are stupid. I am too impatient for dramas. And I don't have time to watch old movies or game shows. (And yes, that's my final answer.)

No, she is talking about my remote control.

And she's right. I do love it. I love it's sleek curves, it's raw functionality. All the cool buttons. (Guys love buttons, even buttons we have no idea how to use. For most of us, Heaven will look like the cockpit of a 747.)

It's also true that I have formed an emotional bond with my remote control that I have not formed with any other mechanical device.

I do not, for instance, love the toaster. I do not love the refrigerator. I do not love the humidifier, the dehumidifier or the smoke detector. Those things are appliances, soul-less utilitarian devices that are but a means to an end.

But my remote control? Ah, now we're talking about something other than a mere widget. A remote control, to a man, is a royal scepter, a magic wand. With it, the world is his.

Click ... The History Channel.
Click ... CNN.
Click ... the sci-fi network.

Past, present, future, plus ESPN for sports. What's not to love?

Women universally fail to understand how we can love a device. I explained it this way the other night to my wife: "Men feel about their remotes the way we feel about our dogs. Both are loyal companions that do our bidding without question. Both never disappoint, barring low batteries. And both deliver untold hours of simple, peaceful pleasure. Name me something or someone else that does all that?"

"I'm sorry," she said. "Did you say something?"

See? No wonder we treat it like it's ours and ours alone. No wonder when one of my children loses the remote, I act like someone has lost, well, one of my children. No wonder when Marcia asks for it, I glare at her suspiciously, like she's trying to steal my socks.

"What are you going to DO with it?" I growl.

"I'm going to pick a program and watch it from end to end just to drive you crazy," she'll reply.

But giving a remote to a woman is like giving a car to a dog. Neither has a practical use for it. Women are born nesters. They want to find a show and snuggle in with it, even to the ridiculous extreme of reading the credits. ("Oh look, honey, Jim Joobydooby was the key grip on this film.") Might as well still walk over to the set and turn a dial.

Men, unless we're talking Super Bowl, are hunters. We roam the fields and woods of the TV landscape always suspecting there's a better show out there somewhere. And if we juuust search hard enough. ...

Or maybe we're just restless. I am. I spin the dial like I'm on "Wheel of Fortune." I always watch more than one program at a time. My record for at-one-sitting viewing is a sitcom, two John Wayne movies, a nature documentary and two football games with side peeks at the dirtier videos on MTV. And the thing is, after I was done, I felt as if I had gotten the gist of each and every one, except of course for that Eminem video. What's the deal with that guy?

And I was able to do it all because of my remote control.

It's a beautiful thing. No other device gives a man such

control. Not a car. Not a power saw. Not a lawn mower. With a remote control, if there's something unpleasant on, you just point, aim, click and, poof, it's gone, replaced by goodness.

I wish the rest of life were like that.

Then again, I also wish the rest of life came with a mute button.

– December 17, 2000

Women should just let it grow

You can't see me, but I'm wearing a black armband here. I am in mourning.

Yes, my wife cut her hair short.

You women are saying, "So?" or possibly "Good for her!"

You men are saying, "We feel your pain, dude," and then giving me that consoling chuck on the arm that men do.

What is it with women? You spend half your lives trying to grow long hair so you will look like the models in the fashion magazines. Then when you near a certain age - for some women it's 30, for some it's 40, for some it's 15 - you suddenly decide "That's it, I've had enough. I'm going short."

And once shorn, you almost never go back.

"Noooooobody knows, the trouble I've seen ..."

Sure, it's great for YOU. And sure, it's cooler and easier to care for and makes you look "sassy" or "cute" or "perky" or whatever term you come up with to justify this crime against nature.

But have you ever considered that we, your loving husbands and boyfriends, have feelings, too? Did it ever occur to you that we want you to have long hair forever and ever and ever?

What about our needs, huh?

Oh, I know. Some men say, "Oh, but I LIKE short hair on women." But they are traitors to the cause. Suck-ups.

Treacherous Eddie Haskells who are merely trying to curry favor.

According to numerous scientific studies about which I will make up convincing details if questioned, males are hard-wired to prefer long-haired women. (You never see a cute bob in Playboy, now do you? Not that we'd notice.)

That's just the way it is. When my wife showed up at home with her long, blond mane chopped short (I say chopped; she calls it a "style"), my 4-year-old daughter squealed, "It's so cuuuuute, Momma."

See, you women, you're all in on it. Even the young ones.

Whereas my 7-year-old son, a male in training, screwed up his nose and said, "Your hair looks weird, Mom. What'dja do?"

This has been the universal reaction. Adult males see her and say matter-of-factly, "Oh, you got your hair cut." Adult females see her and say, in giggly, triumphant terms, as if a blow has just been struck for womanhood, "Oh, you got your hair cut! It looks great!"

"Nooooobody knows my sorrow ..."

My wife knows what I like. So after the deed was done, she called me at work and said, "I got my hair cut short, and if you're smart you'll like it."

So I went home, and I said all of the things I was supposed to say because there's one thing I like better than long hair. (By that I mean clean clothes. What'd you think I meant?)

Plus, you know, I want her to be happy. She says she feels and looks younger and sexier, and who am I to argue? She does look great. But she always looks great. She looked great with long hair. So why couldn't she keep it that way?

"Because I didn't want to," she says. "Now stop being a big baby and go bring in the groceries."

So I went out to bring in the groceries, doing my best to be a kind, supportive husband.

"Noobody knows the troubles I seen ..."

That's when she stuck her head out the door and said, "And for crying out loud, stop singing that song!"

– June 25, 2001

Decoding skills are essential in marriage

I t's time now for another edition of "Ask Dr. Marriage," the unfathomably popular advice column for men mystified by the creatures with whom they share phone bills.

Our question today comes from a close personal friend named Jim Abernathy, who for reasons of anonymity we shall refer to only as "Jim."

Jim asks: "Why is it that I'm supposed to decode what my wife says to me? Why can't she just say what she wants?"

Jim, Jim, Jim. The answer to your question is the same answer I give to all who write Dr. Marriage: Because she's a woman. You might as well ask why the sky is blue or why Carrot Top is quite possibly the most annoying human being ever born.

For some reason, women find it difficult to be blunt as in, "I want you to meet my emotional needs by turning off the football game and listening to me drone on about how my sister wounded my psyche back in the third grade by calling me chunky, and how that comment, that one stupid comment, has haunted me to this day, most recently this morning when I was trying on jeans at the mall."

Instead they'll say, "The dog needs a bath."

The problem with men is that when we hear someone say, "The dog needs a bath," we think, "The dog needs a bath." Which is why we reply, "OK, I'll get to it after the game, honey."

Which, to the woman, is just so totally wrong it's laughable. She's thinking: "What's WRONG with him that he can't see what is so patently obvious to anyone who's paying even the SLIGHTEST bit of attention? Maybe this is a sign that we've finally reached that point in our marriage where the thrill is gone and we just stop communicating. Or maybe this means there's someone else. And maybe he needs someone else because my sister was right and I really AM chunky!"

Which is why she'll begin weeping and say, "I think we need marriage counseling." At which point the man, sensing something is wrong, looks up from the TV and says, "Did you say something, sweetheart?"

To which she says: "I knew something was wrong. I just knew it!" Which startles him, so he says, "OK, I'll go wash the stupid dog now. Sheesh."

Dr. Marriage has encountered this kind of peculiar behavior in his own marriage. The other day Mrs. Dr. Marriage said, and I quote, "I'm going upstairs to read." As a male, Dr. Marriage took that to mean that she was going upstairs. To read.

In fact, Dr. Marriage was wrong, wrong, wrong. What he failed to detect in that simple sentence were the hidden words that followed, as in "I'm going upstairs with a book in my hand not to read but to cool down because your daughter is driving me CRAZY with her moodiness and I'd really appreciate it if you would watch the kids and keep them away from me for a half hour before I scream."

And so Dr. Marriage made a sandwich and turned on the TV. A few minute later, Mrs. Dr. Marriage stomped down the steps and said, "Thanks a lot!" But he could tell she didn't mean thanks a lot.

So he said, "What's wrong? What'd I do?" And she said, "The kids. They followed me right upstairs." Dr. Marriage, sensing impending doom, said sheepishly, "So?"

Mrs. Dr. Marriage's answer took a solid hour, but Dr. Marriage is not entirely sure he understood a word of it.

¬July 26, 2001

Sick wife brings household to standstill

O nce again it's time for "Ask Dr. Marriage," the remarkably popular advice column that has become an oasis of sanity to guys mystified by the creatures with whom they share a toaster.

Today's question comes, as usual, from a close friend of Dr. Marriage's named Bob, who, for reasons of anonymity, we will call "Bill."

Bill writes: "Dear Dr. Marriage: How come when I get sick everything in the house goes on as normal, but when my wife gets sick everything goes straight to hell?"

Bill, Bill, Bill. The answer is obvious: because you are a guy. (This could actually be the answer to all of the questions Dr. Marriage receives.)

Guys never have and never will count as much as women, particularly when it comes to domestic matters. In domestic matters, a second-rate woman is worth five, first-rate guys any day, as any woman will tell you. Think of us as pennies; them as nickels.

Dr. Marriage himself noted this phenomenon in his own household recently.

Dr. Marriage's three kids, one by one, came down with a bizarre combination of the South American Death Flu and God's Own Ear Infection.

And yet, despite being on constant booger patrol (this is where Dr. Marriage abandons all pretense of dignity and straps a roll of toilet paper to his belt), Dr. Marriage's home life proceeded relatively normally.

Then the worst calamity that can befall a guy befell Dr. Marriage: his wife became sick.

Dr. Marriage was at first furious with Mrs. Dr. Marriage, since it clearly states in Article 3, subsection C of their marital contract that, in the event of children, she is not, for any reason, to become ill, disabled or otherwise unable to perform crucial household duties (i.e. "everything.")

But being an understanding guy, Dr. Marriage decided not to declare the marriage null and void and sue her for breach of contract (not to mention pain and suffering). Instead he did his best to make his suffering wife and their suffering children as comfortable as possible.

Unfortunately, his best, in Mrs. Dr. Marriages words, "sucked."

Now understand, Dr. Marriage had no intention to suck at tending the house and taking care of the children. It's just that Dr. Marriage, like many guys, normally lurks on the periphery of usefulness, and so he found these tasks difficult to perform.

For instance, Dr. Marriage learned to his surprise that children need food. Who knew? The problem is that no matter what Dr. Marriage fixed for them they wouldn't eat it because mommy hadn't fixed it. Dr. Marriage eventually solved this problem by propping open the refrigerator.

And then there's the baby. Did you know those things go to the bathroom right in their pants?! Incredible. Dr. Marriage, resourceful one that he is, eventually solved this problem as well, via the skillful employment of a garden hose. Thank goodness it's summer.

The housework, as well, proved to be highly nettlesome. Dr. Marriage quickly learned that his idea of "clean" and his wife's idea of clean did not exactly match.

If you want a mental picture of the state of Dr. Marriage's house after five days, picture a house in Kosovo after the Serbs came through. You know, dead chickens everywhere, walls blown out, filth everywhere.

Now double it.

When his wife questioned him about the mess, Dr. Marriage jokingly suggested that what he needed was a second emergency wife, whom he could keep inside a red case and activate by breaking the glass with a teeny hammer.

He figures he'll stop paying for that remark sometime next century.

– July 8, 1998

We're not lion about true nature of men

I t is a widely held view among women that men are pigs.
How wrong they are.
We're not pigs. We're lions.

I discovered this the other evening when a momentary lapse in my vigilance allowed the lovely yet formidable Marcia to gain control of the clicker.

As usual, she clicked to a nature show. She loves those things. Her favorite is the one where the female spider mates with the male spider then devours him. She laughs at that one like nobody's business. It's kind of eerie, to be honest.

Personally, I hate nature shows. I figure if you've seen one zebra torn to bloody shreds by a snarling pack of hyenas, you've seen them all.

The only nature show I ever liked was Mutual of Omaha's "Wild Kingdom," starring Marlin Perkins. And that was only because Marlin was always making his assistant, Jim, do the dirty work, while he sat safely in a blind doing color commentary. "And now my assistant Jim will attempt to place a radio collar on the angry boa constrictor." "And now my assistant Jim will attempt to remove the painful, cavity-ridden tooth at the back of the tiger's mouth."

I kept waiting for Jim to snap and say, "Stuff it, old man. How about you come down here and HELP ME remove the sleeping grizzly cub from the den of the ill-tempered mother rapidly coming out of sedation, huh?"

But I digress.

This was a show about lions, specifically about what total jerks male lions are. That's not what they said, of course, but that clearly was the upshot. (I bet if I'd watched the credits they would have said, "Paid for by the National Organization for Women.") And it made for quite a lovely evening.

Scene: Female lion going out and killing a water buffalo.

Next scene: Male lion padding up to get first dibs.

Marcia: "Typical. The woman fixes dinner, the man digs in without so much as a thank you. If he were human, he probably wouldn't offer to clean up afterward either."

Me: "Can I have the clicker, please?"

Scene: Female lion carefully feeding and grooming her cubs.

Next scene: Male lion sleeping.

Marcia: "Typical. She works, he sleeps. You seeing any parallels here,

Heller?"

Me (flipping through the TV guide): "Oh, look, ice skating on Channel 28! You love ice skating, don't you, hon?"

Scene: After a full day of chasing the kids, attacking hippos and finding watering holes, the female lion lies down next to the male and tenderly nuzzles his mane.

Next scene: Male lion sneaking off just before dawn to visit the family he has with another female on the other side of the valley.

Marcia: "You see that! He left her! Just up and left her! She's stuck with the kids and he goes off to satisfy his `needs.' God, what IS it with men? Why can't you just be happy with what you've got?"

Me: "Um, uh, you see ..."

Scene: Male lion with his other family. Sleeping.

Next scene: Female lion seeming a bit lonely for her mate, but otherwise doing OK.

Marcia: "See! She doesn't need him! She's doing just fine. You go, girl!"

At this point, I'm employing the male marital survival technique known as keeping your mouth shut.

Scene: A month later, the male lion comes back.

Personally, I was expecting a blowout. I was expecting the female to rip off his head and feed it to the cubs. Instead, she warmly welcomed him as if nothing had happened, then trotted off to kill an antelope for his dinner.

Marcia frowned. I tried to stifle a smile.

"Shut up," she growled.

¬*June 14, 1997*

What the world needs is two Andys

Now that scientists have cloned sheep, many think it's only a matter of time before they clone people.

So I said to my wife, the lovely yet formidable Marcia: "How about if I get myself cloned? You know, like the sheep."

"No, thanks," she said. "You're more than enough man for me, sweetie."

"Why, thank you."

"Although the idea is kind of amusing," she continued, with a little snort of a laugh. "I mean, really, two of you? I'd go crazy."

"Hey!"

"I'm sorry, dear," she said, patting my leg. "But it's true."

"Oh, and how is it true?" I growled.

"Well, since you asked, we only have the one couch."

"So?"

"So, it would never work. One couch, two men. Where would Andy II plop his keister every Sunday, all Sunday?"

"Har de har har."

"And, of course, if there were two of you I'd have to buy a machete to hack through all the guy grunge in the bathroom."

"Guy grunge?"

"You know, whiskers in the sink, toenail clippings on the floor. And don't get me started about the toilet, Mr. Lousy

Aim."

"My aim is just fine," I said. "And those aren't my toenails. They can't be. I very carefully and pointedly toss my clipped toenails in the wastebasket."

"Oh, then whose toenails are they?"

"That's just what I was going to ask you," I said. "Maybe you've been inviting the mailman in for a little hanky-panky and foot grooming."

"Oh, please. That's the best you can do? You know they're yours. Just admit it."

"Sorry. That's my story and I'm sticking to it. And stop rolling your eyes like that."

"I can't help it," she said. "It's an involuntary reflex brought on by exposure to bull hooey."

I chose, as is my wont, to take the high road and ignore that insult.

"Really, honey," I said. "Two of me would be wonderful. Just think, the work around the house would get done twice as fast."

"Tell me," she said, folding her arms. "What's two times nothing?"

"Uh, zero," I answered.

"Then cloning you wouldn't get the work done any faster since it's not getting done now."

"That's not true! Why, just the other day, I hung that picture you wanted hung."

"I asked you to hang that picture six months ago!"

"I was mentally preparing myself."

"Uh-huh. And how about the weather-stripping I've been after you since November to put around the front door?"

"I'm waiting for warmer weather. You want me to freeze?"

"But we need it now, while it's cold. Do you want your family to freeze?"

"Only sometimes," I said.

She frowned a frown only an experienced wife can frown. "What we need," she said, "is to clone me. Then we'd see some action around here."

I thought about it for a minute. Two Marcias. Hmmm. Twice the back rubs. Twice the snow shoveling.

And twice the ...

"What are you ..." she began. "Oh, god, you are such a pig.

What is it with men? You can turn anything into sex."

"Not true," I said. "When we talk about batting averages, the subject of sex never once comes up."

Her eyes rolled again.

"So what I'm hearing is that cloning is out, correct?" I asked.

"No, not cloning entirely. Just cloning you. I wouldn't mind at all having a few of those cloned sheep."

"Sheep?" I said. "What in the world for?"

"You know, so the lawn gets cut regularly."

–March 2, 1997

Orange juice is a sticky topic

f my marriage ever ends it will be the orange juice's fault. Well. Actually. It will be my wife's fault because she's always screwing up the orange juice, but I can't very well say that because if I do she'll get mad, so I won't.

But I am already off my point.

I was thirsty, so I went to the refrigerator and pulled out the blue plastic pitcher in which we keep the orange juice. We make our own.

No. Not fresh-squeezed. Are you kidding? We use those hard, nasty tubes of orange juice you get in the frozen food section instead of the tasty, convenient juice that comes pre-mixed in plastic jugs.

We use them because Marcia does the shopping, and she says they are cheaper. And when the person in the house who doesn't do the shopping complains about it, she hands him a list and matter-of-factly says, "Here you go. And don't forget the diapers." So the person who doesn't do the shopping rarely opens his mouth.

Still, he is not a fan of the tubes. For one thing, food should not come rolled in a tube. Aren't you glad other food products don't come like that? You ought to be. Can you imagine tubed, frozen liver?

Then there's the fact that the tubes are hard to open. You can spend a long time opening one of them.

The plastic band that you pull to release the end of the can

frequently rips, so you have to use a can opener. But a can
opener doesn't work very well because the tubes weren't
designed to be opened that way.

So the would-be juice drinker wrestles with it at length, all
the while slopping sticky concentrate all over his hands and
trousers, forcing him to vent his frustration via long strings of
bad words.

Then, when he finally gets it open, he shakes the tube over
the blue plastic pitcher, but the cylinder of orange gunk
doesn't come out because his freezer only has two settings,
not-cold-enough and North Pole.

So he either ends up jamming a knife in there to pry it
loose, another messy job. Or he peels away the cardboard
container along the seams, the way you do with those instant
biscuit tubes.

It's a very involved, goopy process. All for a lousy glass of
juice.

But back to our story.

I poured myself a tall glass of juice, and right away I
noticed something was wrong. The juice was thin. A weak,
pale orange, like the orange of a winter sun, not the hearty,
deep orange of a summer sun.

I tasted it. It tasted the same as it looked. Thin. Weak.
Palsied. It was like Tang. Only without the nine essential
vitamins and minerals.

I knew who was responsible because she's always
responsible. Marcia is a good woman. She loves me (a true
sign of good womanhood). She loves the kids. She's good at
cribbage.

But - and I'm sorry to have to say this, but it's true - she is
a lazy orange juice maker. Instead of pouring exactly three
tubes of water into the pitcher, as per the instructions, she
holds the pitcher under the tap and guesstimates the amount
of water needed.

The predictable result: orange juice that is either too
strong or too weak, never just right. And an upset juice-
drinking husband.

"Why, oh why, can't you just measure it?" he sometimes
moans.

"Sorry," she says. "But if you don't like it, you could make
it for once, you know."

"I wouldn't have to make it if you'd stop buying frozen," he replies.

"Here you go," she says, handing over the grocery list. "And don't forget the diapers."

Sigh. Marriage.

Good thing she's good at cribbage.

–November 17, 1997

The Young and the Restless

Let's get a few things straight, kid

My son and I had a conversation the other day. It was an admittedly one-sided conversation because he is just a year old. But it was time I had a few things out with him.

"Son, I'm sure you're wondering why I called this little meeting."

"Bweee!"

"But before I begin, let me assure you that your mother and I love you more than anything in the world, with the possible exception of cookie dough ice cream."

"Gurgle."

"OK, OK, we love you more than cookie dough ice cream. But there are a few issues concerning your behavior that ... hey, come back here."

"Bubbabubbabubba."

"That's better. Now, as I was saying, your mother and I feel that while you are a wonderful baby, there are a few teensy-weensy areas you need to work on. Sleeping, for instance. We feel that since you haven't slept for more than four seconds at a time your whole, entire life, maybe you haven't totally grasped the concept. So we have prepared the following multiple choice test.

"Listen carefully. When we put you in your crib, are you supposed to: A) Scream so loudly the neighbors think we're strangling a goat with piano wire; B) Reluctantly fall asleep, making sure to wake every hour on the hour until dawn like a pint-sized vampire in footie pajamas; or C) Drift peacefully off to sleep and remain in that state until "Regis & Kathie Lee" comes on the next morning so your mommy and daddy don't stumble around acting as if they've been main-lining antihistimines."

"DADADADADA!"

"Good boy! Now about your dining habits. I know breast-feeding is a wonderful, natural, beautiful thing. But enough's enough, kiddo. You simply can't go through your whole life attached to your mommy's, uh, you know, her, um, mommary glands. When you get to junior high school, kids'll talk."

"Bop bop bop."

"Besides, have you ever heard of `hormones?'"

"MAMAMAMAMA!"

"Well, it's like this, son: Mommy's moods are under the evil influence of these things called hormones."

"Duhwee?"

"I know, I was amazed, too. But she swears it's true. These hormones apparently make her say things like, `Not tonight, dear,' and `What, again? Has it been a month already?' Daddy hates hormones, Sam."

"DEEDEEEDEE!"

"The point is, if you want a little brother or sister I suggest you switch to moo-moo juice reeeeal soon, OK?"

"Bububub."

"Great! Then there's the matter of your teeth. Maybe you don't know this, but God didn't give you teeth so you could gnaw the legs of the dining room chairs. Repeat after me, son: Wood is for beavers."

"Weh weh weh."

"Good. Let's see, what else? Ah, yes, mommy and daddy don't think it's funny when you squirt like a cherub fountain at Versailles the second your diaper's removed. We realize that if you were older you would probably get a large National Endowment for the Arts grant for this behavior, but we're tired of wringing out your teddy bear, so knock it off, OK?"

"Blumblumblum."

"I'm also sick of `Pat the Bunny.' Can we dump that?"

"Blumblumblum."

"Good. And Raffi. Daddy hates Raffi, Sam. Wouldn't you

like to listen to some nice, smokey jazz instead?"

"Muhmuhmuhmuh."

"Wonderful! I'm glad you're taking this so well. But be straight with me, son ..."

"DADADADA!"

"There's not a chance in heck you're going to change any of the stuff we've talked about today, is there?"

"Wheeeeedeedee!"

"Didn't think so."

–March 13, 1995

Why oh why do kids ask why?

I had the following fascinating discussion with my son the other night.

Me: "Sam, could you bring me that towel over there?"

Sam: "Why?"

Me: "Because I want to wipe your sister's face."

Sam: "Why?"

Me: "Because she spit up a little bit."

Sam: "Why?"

Me: "Because her stomach is upset."

Sam: "Why?"

Me: "Because she ate too fast."

Sam: "Why?"

Me: "Because she was hungry."

Sam: "Why?"

Me: "Because she hadn't eaten in two hours."

Sam: "Why?"

Me: "Because she was napping."

Sam: "Why?"

Me: "Because she was tired."

Me: "Because ... look, would you please stop asking why?"

Sam: "Why?"

Me: "Because you're driving me crazy!"

Sam: "Why?"

Me: "Because answering all of these questions is

annoying!"

Sam: "Why?"

Me: "BECAUSE IT JUST IS!"

Sam: "Why?"

Me: "Because ... because many questions, in the existential sense of things, are ultimately unanswerable, and attempting to answer the unanswerable inevitably causes your poor father great mental frustration, which causes his blood pressure to rise, which causes a rapid twitching in his left eye. OK? Now can I have the stupid towel, please?"

He stopped to think about that for a moment. Then he looked up at me with his big brown eyes and said, "Why?"

There's no winning with a 3-year-old.

My wife and I are beginning to think this whole talking thing is overrated.

When Sam was a baby we couldn't WAIT for him to say his first word: "C'mon," we'd urge. "Say Daddy! Say Mommy!"

He'd usually respond by making spit bubbles, which was thrilling enough. But every now and then, through the bubbles, would come a profound utterance, something along the lines of "uh-bleah-bleah," which would cause us to ooh and aah with such force that you'd swear fireworks had just gone off in the living room.

"Wow! That was `Daddy,' clear as day!"

I remember us talking about how wonderful it would be when, someday, Sam would be able to express his deepest wants, needs and feelings. And now that he can express these things, we can't get him to shut up. Especially with this why stuff, which just all of a sudden happened.

Why?

I don't know. He's a kid. Kids are just that way.

Why?

Stop it.

Look. We want to be good parents. We want to indulge and nurture his curiosity about things bla bla bla. And we do. We try to answer. But sometimes there's no end. The other day, Marcia counted.

"Eighteen whys!" she said. "Eighteen!"

The conversation, she said, started out to be about why he should pick up his train set and ended up a half hour later and approximately 47 miles off course on the topic of clouds and why they're white.

Anyway, we are told this is just a stage, that there will come a time when he will not ask "why" every 16 seconds.

We are also told there is a stage ahead when his verbal skills will, in fact, regress, and he will become so silent and uncommunicative that we will begin to wonder if his vocal cords have been removed.

This wondrous stage, apparently, is called "the teen-age years."

Frankly, we can't wait.

–April 7, 1997

Training wheels come off way too soon

I am in the street in front of my home helping my son learn to ride his bike without training wheels.

He is equal parts excited and terrified.

As I jog down the street beside him, my hand steadying his wobbles, he yelps, "Don't let go, daddy! Don't let go!"

Here is what I am thinking: I won't, Sam. I won't. I'll never let go.

But I know someday soon that I will. He'll want me to. He'll suddenly find his balance and, zoom, he'll be gone. Flying. Without me.

That will be one of the proudest, saddest days of my life.

I admit it. I am an overly emotional father. I am guilty of seeing him try to ride his first real bike and thinking that this is the start of his freedom, his independence from me and his mother.

Next he'll be riding that bike around the block. Then to the next block over to visit friends from school. (School!)

Then, between blinks, he'll be asking me to teach him how to drive. (Downshift! Downshift!) The next thing you know he'll be borrowing the car for dates. Then, finally, the day will come when he leaves home for good. A bird freely flown.

These thoughts, this racing ahead, doesn't even seem ludicrous to me anymore. How strange this parenting. I used to be largely indifferent to the idea of children. I delayed it for the first 10 years of our marriage. Despite Marcia's desires. In order to play. I grew up in a large family and wasn't ready for a full house yet. I treasured my free time, my independence.

Then came Sam. He is 4 now. And I can't imagine life now without him.

I'm not just saying that. I really can't. I try to conjure my life before he showed up. The parties. The movies. The concerts. The weekend getaways. The fun we had. And the thoughts seem somehow unreal. We so infrequently do any of those things now, it seems almost as if that were somebody else.

And yet ...

And yet I wouldn't trade my now life for my then life for anything. Who knew I'd like the kid so much? Who knew I'd reach a point in my life where a part of me wished against hope that my son would stop growing up.

But there I am. There we are. Marcia and I look at him one minute and he is the same Sam we've always known. The next, we'll look at him and see him as if through a prism. There's something different. Ever so slightly. I catch a glimpse of the man yet to be.

I love that glimpse. I hate that glimpse.

"I wish he would stay this age forever," I'll say to Marcia.

I said that when he was a baby. I said it when he was 2. I said it when he was 3. And now that he's nearly 5 I'm saying it again. Stop, time, stop.

But of course there is no stopping time. There never was.

I remember my father, always so busy with jobs and chores and committees that there was never enough time for his six children.

I wanted so badly for time to stop then so he would eventually finish those other things and be with us.

We needed him. He was a good man. He loved us. I know that. But I don't know if my dad, who is gone now, ever needed me the way I need Sam.

I feel all of this as I'm jogging down the street beside him, encouraging Sam to go, go, go, to learn, to ride that bike.

But in truth I hope he takes his own sweet time about it.

I want him to need me for just a little while longer.

–October 11, 1998

The real world is suddenly too close

The man on the TV was talking about the school shooting in California.

Sam, my 7-year-old son, who was watching the news with us because we want him to develop an interest in the world, turned to his mother and said, "Momma, where's California?"

"Far, far away from here," she replied, trying to sound comforting.

The man on the TV talked about how the shooter was only 15 and had been teased a lot by the other kids and how he used his daddy's gun.

"Momma," Sam said. "What grade is he in?"

"Ninth grade, dear."

"Will I be in ninth grade?"

Not for a long time, I thought. Sweet Mary and Joseph, not for a long, long time.

There are times when you shrink as a parent, times when you stop being tall enough to see over counters and remember what it was like to be a kid, knee-high to a scary, scary world that you don't quite understand.

This was one of those moments. We could hear in his voice what was going through his head: "Will they shoot me at MY school? Is this what growing up is like? What if they tease me like that?"

And it just about breaks your heart.

I wanted to grab him and hug him and tell him, "No, sweetie, no. No one's going to shoot you and no one's going to tease you and your entire school career will be safe and uneventful and your whole life, too."

But I didn't say that because I worried that by trying not to scare him I would scare him.

Plus, I know it's not true. The world IS a scary place. It's a world where everyone has guns or can get guns. And unlike in my childhood, they aren't afraid to use guns.

It's also a world where they tease you in school. But it has always been that way. They tease the fat and the ugly. They tease the kid with acne and the kid who is quiet. They tease and tease and tease anyone who stands out for any reason.

In the shooter's case, they teased him about being skinny and shy and pale. No one knows yet whether that's what caused him to snap, but if that was it, if it even contributed a little bit, would you be surprised?

I worry on several levels about this. I was terribly skinny. I was teased, and I remember how much it hurt. Sam will probably be the same way. I can see it in him. He's skinnier than a rail. But he's feisty and outgoing, unlike his father was. So maybe it will be all right. Maybe they'll leave him alone.

And maybe - just maybe - all of these shootings will teach parents to get rid of their guns and to talk to their kids about not teasing other kids. Maybe parents will tell their children to tell them when one of their friends threatens to do something violent and not just assume he's joking.

But I doubt it. It didn't happen after Columbine. So why would it happen now? The world is the world. People rarely learn.

And so I as I watch my son - my Sam - trudge off to the bus stop, his Digimon backpack dangling off one arm, one leg of his snowpants hiked up on his boot, I try to mentally project a cocoon of safety around him, a cocoon that no tease, no taunt, no bullet can penetrate.

It's not much, but it's the best I can do in a scary, scary world.

–March 7, 2001

Parents get the yellow bus blues

I am standing with the other neighborhood parents in a driveway down the block in the early morning chill.

We are full of smiles and easy, good-natured conversation despite the fact that we are all, I suspect, dying inside.

At least I am.

The school bus is coming to get my Sam for his first full day of kindergarten, and there's nothing I can do about it, even if I wanted to.

This is a good thing, after all. The moment that bus wheezes to a stop, opens its door and swallows him up, that's really the start of his future.

From here on in, the years will be a blur: kindergarten, middle school, high school, college, job, marriage, kids of his own. This is it: the jumping off point.

Maybe that's what's causing my breath to be short, as if someone has cinched a rope around my chest. The swoop and sweep of it all is dizzying, too big a gulp of life to swallow at one time.

This is inside stuff, of course. On the outside I am joking with the other parents, filming the whole scene with my video camera, treating it all like it's no big deal.

Another dad, Dan, comes out and teases the moms.

"Get ready to cry," he says.

The moms say, "Oh, stop," smiling at the recognition of

their tension.

The children, of course, are oblivious to such ridiculous adult feelings. They are yelping and whining and laughing in a swirl around us, just as always. Sam, his face shining, his Power Rangers pack strapped to his back over his Scooby Doo wind-breaker, my whole universe in his eyes, doesn't seem nervous at all.

And why should he be? Kids don't waste time on "momentous" occasions. They don't see life as a whole. They see only the small part of it actually before them. That's the secret to their joy.

Then, too, we have spent weeks preparing him for this moment. He's been on several practice runs on the bus. He knows all the rules. No standing, no pushing, no pinching, no yelling. Listen to the bus driver. Never cross in front of the bus after you get out.

He knows the rules for school, too. No talking out of turn, no pushing, no pinching, listen to the teacher, pay attention.

About the only thing we haven't covered with him are the things I most want say: "If a kid picks on you, please don't let it scar you. Please don't take it to heart, as I know you will."

Or: "Please remember that you are the most special little kid in the whole wide world, and don't let the big, bad world harm you or scare you or change you in any way."

The bus is coming now, and my heart leaps. This is it. It's going to scoop him up and take him away from us, from me.

For the first time, he'll be alone, on his own. The thought of it is as alien to me as my liver leaping out of my abdomen and going for a walk on its own. And I have to keep repeating to myself: this is a good thing, this is a good thing.

Without a backward glance, Sam hops on the bus with the other kids. To my regret, he chooses an aisle seat, not a window seat, so it is hard for him to see me waving.

The bus pulls away and I follow it with the lens of my camera.

"Keep going! Keep going!" I joke aloud for the other parents and for this videotaped posterity.

But inside I am wishing that it would stop now, let out my perfect son, and never, ever come back.

– August 5, 1999

Weathering emotional storm Annie

I have been married a long, long time to a woman who is all but Helen Reddy's sister in the "I am woman, hear me roar" department.

So I normally do not speak in sweeping generalizations when it comes to the female gender because: A) I have learned over the years that there are absolutely no differences between males and females except for the obvious body parts, and B) My wife will slug me hard on the meat of the arm if I do.

But this one time I must indulge in a generalization: Girls are tougher to raise than boys. At least for fathers.

There. I said it.

I've thought it for years. And I suspect many fathers would say they agree with me if it weren't for the fact that they, too, are tired of having sore arms.

I have three children: a 6-year-old boy, a 1-year-old boy and Annie.

Annie is 3. I adore her. I dote on her. I will give you an example of why I think she is scarier to raise than the boys.

The other night, Annie was cold so she crawled into bed with us. Morning came and I noticed her next to me, so I rolled over and began whispering to her.

"I love you, sweetie," I burbled. "You're the best girl in the whooole world."

She looked at me, rolled over to her mother and said,

"Daddy's talking to me again."

She said this in an extremely annoyed tone, as if I had spent the entire night babbling to her about macroeconomics and its impact on the current presidential race.

Marcia, who thinks she is very, very funny, hugged Annie and said, "I know, honey. He's a bad, bad daddy."

Annie said "Hmmph!" and folded her arms.

My daughter: the 3-year-old teen-ager.

"Just wait until she's an actual teen-ager," says Marcia. "Then she'll say, `Daddy's breathing again, mom.'"

What mystifies my kind the most about girls - and by my kind I mean stupid fathers - are all the emotions. Annie can become extremely emotional about anything: a Barbie dress that won't go on, a molecule of crust left on her peanut butter and jelly sandwich, the weather.

I walked into the room the other day - just walked in - and Annie crumpled to the floor and began crying.

"What? What?" I said, startled. "What'd I do?"

Marcia, who was in a chair leafing through a magazine, said, "She's just having emotions."

"Having emotions?" I said. "About what?"

"I don't know. Does there have to be a reason?"

Well, yes. Guys have emotions in response to things. If, for instance, I spill a beer at the ballpark, I cry. If someone cuts me off in traffic, I get angry.

But I have talked to numerous fathers about this and many, many of them say that their daughters have emotions the way Kansas has twisters. They pop up out of nowhere, for no apparent reason, they blow hard and fast, then they're gone. Two minutes after Annie was done having her emotions, she was on my lap giggling and tickling me.

"I will never understand your kind," I said to Marcia.

She just laughed.

I'm not sure what she meant by that. But there's no way in heck I'm asking.

– August 18, 2000

Snow is the stuff of a young girl's dreams

I awoke Monday to the first snow of the year - a great, white, dismal, gloppy mess.

"Super," I sighed, looking groggily out the window at it, envisioning all of the work and bother it would cause me.

I'll have to shovel, I grumbled. Shoveling is a pain, but I refuse to get a snowblower because that would be an admission that I just can't hack it anymore.

I'll have to salt, too. That's the last thing I need - a UPS guy falling on the steps and suing me.

Oh, man, and I'll have to find my shoes to fetch the paper in the driveway, too. Hate that. Normally, I dash out barefoot. I miss the days when kids delivered the paper and they put it right inside your screen door. Nothing's as good as it used to be.

And of course I'll have to go hunt up an old towel to wipe the dog's feet. If I don't she'll track glop and gunk all over the carpets when she comes in. Stupid dog. Dogs are a pain, too.

And, naturally, I'll have to scrape the windows of my car, since I haven't gotten around to cleaning the summer stuff out of my spot in the garage.

Then I'll have to give myself extra time to get to work because all the morons who don't know how to drive in bad weather will be either going too fast and end up in the ditch or too slow and get in my way.

By the time I finished my laundry list of bad, bad things

that the weather would bring, I had made myself pretty miserable.

Then my daughter, the wild and untameable Annie, came flying into the room.

"It snowed!" she cried. "It snowed! I want go outside!"

"Honey, it's 6:30 in the morning. You can't ..."

But she was already gone, racing down the stairs to find her mother.

"Put my boots on!" I heard her say.

So Marcia put her boots on her, and her jacket and her snowpants and her hat and her mittens, and out into the dark, snowy chill she zipped. The last I looked, she was out there brushing the snow off my car as high up as she could reach, which is about the height of the door handles.

My daughter is 3, incidentally. That means she still has that light in her eyes that adults always wish they still had. Eyes that allow her to see beauty as beauty and opportunity as opportunity.

And that's why I feel like an idiot today.

I frequently forget what my children have always known - that the world is a wonderful, magical place.

I'm like many adults. I'm blessed with experience and intelligence about the world, so I am able to see things coming a long way off. I know that snow means extra work, which means extra time lost in a long, busy day, which means more fatigue and stress, which ... .

At least I think it's a blessing. I wonder sometimes. Children have small telescopes. They don't look that far out. They see what's before them. They see snow. They remember that snow means sloshing around outside. And that sloshing around outside is fun. That's it. End of analysis.

Perhaps it's they who are blessed. If so, at least they share it from time to time.

After she came inside, her cheeks red, her nose dripping, Annie looked at me and said with all the wisdom of the universe: "Snow is wunnerful, daddy."

So, my sweet, are 3-year-old girls.

– December 8, 1999

Birth class is no place for the squeamish

Here I am. In birthing class. Sitting on a hard plastic chair. Under harsh fluorescent lights. And here is what I am thinking: "I wish I hadn't had spaghetti for dinner."

Birthing class isn't the place you want to be if you just ate something colorful, especially if you have a weak stomach.

On a scale of one to 10, my stomach is Don Knotts.

I feel bad about this. Marcia is profoundly, eminently, beautifully pregnant. She's a month from delivering our third child. She needs me to be strong. To help her through this.

But when it comes to anything involving pain or bodily fluids, even if they aren't mine, I am what in highly technical medical terminology is known as a "shaking, quaking, simpering, whimpering weenie-wimp."

So when the instructor says - as she inevitably does; there's no stopping her - "... and if the baby tears the mother on the way out, what they do is take a needle and ..." I begin to tense up faster than Carmen Electra's father when she said, "Dad, meet my new husband, Dennis Rodman."

I hate needles. I can't imagine having a needle inserted into me "down there." And I really can't imagine what it must be like to tear yourself down there.

Wait. Yes. I can. I just did, dammit. Ow. And now here is what I am thinking: "Why on earth did I also have a side of corn?"

There are lots of needles in childbirth. And women voluntarily ask to be stuck with them. In the spine! And this is supposed to EASE their pain!

I can't imagine the magnitude of the pain I'd have to be in to request a needle in the spine. But it would be pretty bad. Say, simultaneous Charlie horses in each calf.

I don't even know why I had to come to class this time. It's not as if I could possibly forget this stuff from the first two times. Believe me, I have tried. Unfortunately, it is seared into all of my lobes and possibly my brain stem. You would also think I would get better at this. That I would calm down a bit. But, no. I am actually worse because this is a "refresher" course for veteran parents. It is a two-night, condensed version of the original six-week class, which means the gory stuff comes quicker.

"Let's talk about Caesarians," says the instructor, cheerfully. "Now, as you can see in these incredibly detailed full-color drawings and photographs guaranteed to frighten the hell out of you, it is an agonizing, gut-wrenching, bloody process."

OK, she didn't say that. But she does show photos. Lots and lots of messy photos and horrifying drawings. Who designed this course, Stephen King?

"Now let's talk about the afterbirth ..." she says. "Here are some more disturbing, nightmare-inducing photos."

Yup. Definitely Stephen King.

I particularly hate the afterbirth discussion. I know the placenta is a natural and beautiful part of a natural and beautiful process, but for god's sake I had broccoli for dinner, too.

I say to my wife: "Honey, I don't feel so good. Maybe I should go wait in the lobby."

She whispered back, "I'm the one who's going to give birth here, you know."

Believe me, I know. If I had to give birth, we would be childless. I am weak. Women are strong. I would not trade places with them. Not for one second. That's why, when I go to birthing class, I always end up being thankful for two things.

One, that God made me a man.

And two, that I didn't have tapioca for dessert.

–December 13, 1998

There's no mistaking perfection

Our pediatrician asked us once if we planned to have another child.

We had two at the time.

"No way," we both said. Been there, done that, changed enough diapers, had enough sleepless nights.

He looked at me and said, "So, you must be getting a vasectomy then, right?" Wrong, I said. No one's going to be neutering this dog. That would be like defacing the Mona Lisa, parking a Maserati in the garage, hobbling Man O' War, telling Mark McGwire to bunt. I couldn't in good conscience deprive femaledom, much less my wife, of me, in all my fertile glory.

He laughed.

"Oh, you'll have another baby, all right. Third babies are almost always oops babies."

We laughed back. Us? A third child? Ridiculous. We're adults. We're careful. We're ...

Oops.

His name is Henry James.

The James part comes from the lovely yet formidable Marcia's father. It was set in stone, at the lovely yet formidable Marcia's insistence, minutes after we found out he was coming. I think she might have held to it even if he had been a she, even if it meant turning James into Jamie.

The Henry part we just liked. The combination,

accidentally, makes the name of the author of "The Turn of the Screw." Put your own joke here. Our pediatrician certainly will.

As with our other children, we prefer to think Henry chose to have us rather than us unintentionally making him.

His soul was floating out there in the great ethereal beyond, searching the world below for suitable parents.

One day (or whatever they call it up there) he looked down, spied us and thought, "Hmm. Those two look too rested."

And that was that.

Too rested has become hollow eyed. Silence has become a memory. The 3 a.m. television lineup has become familiar once again. And the comfortable rhythm we had fallen into with the kids has been blown to smithereens. Henry James has become the pea under our mattress.

It's nice.

Lives, like soup stocks, need a good stirring from time to time.

The question everyone asks is: Is he sleeping?

The answer is yes. But at the wrong times. For us. He sleeps through the din of the day, as the loud and unruly Sam and the wild and untameable Annie whoop and holler around him.

Then as night falls and the house quiets, bing, he's awake, just in time for full attention.

Smart kid.

The other big question: How do the kids like him?

They like him fine. Almost too fine. They pet him. I think they think he's a puppy. And he is, in a sense. He's cute, squiggly, has a cold nose, doesn't speak and pees and poops wherever and whenever he pleases.

They speak to him like a puppy, too. "Smile, Henry. Come on, smile." I hope it ends by the time he's older, though. "Here, Henry. Come here. Good Henry. Sit, boy, sit." No, that wouldn't be good for his ego.

He has especially endeared himself to Sam. The other day during a changing, he did what little boys and only little boys are capable of doing, all over himself and the carpet. We call him Fountain Boy. Sam, who is 4, thought it was hysterical and wants to try it himself.

Uh, thanks kid, but no.

All in all, things are great. He couldn't be cuter. We couldn't be happier.

And despite how he came to be, we have already decided that he is not our oops baby, after all. Oops means someone made a mistake.

Henry James is no mistake.

He is beauty itself.

¬January 25, 1999

Clearly, babies want to kill themselves

E veryone thinks babies are such happy creatures.
They certainly appear happy a lot of the time, with their cherubic faces and angelic smiles.

But I believe there is a dark side to these small humans. I think inside they are seething stews of dissatisfaction who resent the fact that we plucked them from the ether and brought them to this plane of existence with all its inherent problems of greed and avarice and wet, uncomfortable diapers.

That's why they keep trying to return to whence they came by killing themselves.

I kid you not. I have three young children. The first two in their baby days exhibited clear suicidal tendencies. And now, Henry, my third and last child, is as well. He is 10 months old. From all appearances he is a happy kid. You look at him, you see a Gerber baby. Round, smiling face. Cute little tooth making its way up from his bottom gum. Constant coos and gurgles. He's a Hollywood typecast.

So why, I wonder, all the suicide attempts?

He has two methods of choice. The first is flinging himself off of things, particularly his high chair.

I'll be sitting there feeding him pureed turkey mixed with apple, turn my head for a second - one second! - to look at something across the room (often something like my 3-year-old daughter attempting to perform oral surgery on the puppy with a plastic fork from her Barbie kitchen), and when I turn back around, Henry has worked his way up out of the seat and is now attempting to fling himself to the ground. (Yes, we strap him in. The kid's Houdini.)

The kid simply wants to fall. We turn our heads, boom, he climbs up on the couch. Then comes the swan dive. We turn our heads, he climbs the steps. Swan dive. We turn our heads, he's on the hearth. Swan dive with a half twist.

In each instance, the second we spot him we become cartoon parents, our legs spinning furiously, exclamation points of panic flying from our skulls. We've become experts at diving catches spectacular enough to make Ken Griffey Jr. envious.

Henry's reaction is always the same. He smiles, then goes off to look for other ways to injure himself. (And before you say it, yes, we've heard of playpens. But my wife, the lovely yet formidable Marcia, believes in free-range children. Don't ask me why. If I had my way, children would be Velcroed to the wall.)

Henry's other method of choice is choking.

He's one of those kids with the unique ability to sense the presence of small, potentially fatal items on the floor. Not just see. Sense. He'll be sitting there playing (for a change) with one of his authorized toys, when he'll stop, swivel his head the way a dog does when it hears some far off sound, then he'll go tearing off.

We'll follow him, naturally, because we know by now that he has sensed the presence of something consumable, say, a marble that my 5-year-old son dropped on the floor a week ago and has since been kicked under an end table.

Henry's intent is clear: "I'm going to crawl over there, jam that marble in my mouth and leave this veil of tears."

We catch him in time every time. We are extremely vigilant parents. Still, it's troubling, this tendency of his.

The only cure, we know, is time.

"That's just how babies are," other, more experienced parents tell us. "Until they get a little older, babies just do that stuff. They ought to be in strait-jackets."

OK, I understand. But here's my question:

How did the human race get so big?

–November 22, 1999

Don't make me come back there

'm sure you're dying to know how my recent family vacation went, which is why I have prepared the following slide show:

Shh-shink

That's me in the captain's chair of our family minivan peering into the back as we prepare to depart on a 10-day drive across the state, which will include an eight-hour journey to my hometown in the Upper Peninsula. You can see how rested and relaxed I appear. Look. I'm even smiling.

Shh-shink

That pale, gooey creature there, that's my 3-year-old daughter. She has just answered my question. I asked, "So, are we all set to go?" She answered with a resounding "BLOOORP!"

Throwing up is the traditional start of any long car trip in our family. It's like the lighting of the Olympic torch. It sort of kicks things off.

Usually, however, we make it out of the driveway first.

Shh-shink

That's me again a half hour into the trip. I am walking my 6-year-old son into a rest stop bathroom. This is another family vacation tradition with us. Before we leave, I say in a stern, fatherly voice, "So does anybody have to go? Because I'm not stopping. I mean it this time. No stopping." And they all say no. And then we end up stopping at each and every rest stop between home and where we're going. The farthest we've ever made it before the kids are overcome with a severe case of urinositosis is, I think, 35 miles. But that's only because they fell asleep.

Shh-shink

That's me again. That look of frustration on my face is because I have just said for the 4,567,232nd time "No, we're not there yet." I should note that at this point we are only two hours into the trip.

Shh-shink

That trembling wretch there, that's my wife, the lovely yet formidable Marcia. She has that gaunt, haunted look on her face because she has spent the last four hours wedged between my daughter's car seat and the baby's car seat trying to stop the baby from wailing. The baby, unfortunately, does not feel the need to stop wailing. He is sick of being in his car seat and he wants everyone within a three-mile radius to know it.

Shh-shink

That's me again. You can see from the expression on my face that I am close to snapping. The kids have decided that to pass the time they will torture one another in various ways, both physical and psychological.

It goes like this:

Sam: "Daaddy (pinch), Annie's (pinch, pinch) pulling my hair."

Me: "Stop it."

Annie: "Daaddy (blowing raspberries), one molecule of Sam's finger is on my side of the seat!"

Me: "Stop it."

Sam: "Daaaaaaaddy (administering a wet willie), Annie called me a poo-poo head."

Me: (Sound of weeping)

Shh-shink

That's me again, this time in full snap. You can't tell from this slide but I have become my father. I am hauling out all of his best lines, including "Don't make me stop this car," "Do I have to come back there? Huh? Do I?" and the immortal "When we get to grandma's house, there's going to be big trouble!"

Car vacations: God's way of telling you to stay the heck home where you belong.

¬*June 12, 2000*

Joining this club is a real pain

The worst part about getting a vasectomy is, let's not kid anyone, the procedure itself.

Knives and that part of the male anatomy just don't mix. (In fact, I'm having an awful flashback right now.) (Ow.)

But the second worst part is having to explain for days on end how it went.

"So ..." people will say to me, trying hard not to glance down there.

"So what?" I'll reply.

"So how'd it go?"

"It went."

"Did it hurt?"

"Yes, it hurt."

"A lot?"

"Some."

"Are you walking funny?"

"No, funnier than before."

"So no more lead in the pencil."

"Nope."

"No more bullets in the gun."

"I guess not."

"No more caffeine in the coffee. No more ink in the pen. No more ..."

"Uh, listen, can I order now?"

It's been almost that bad. I know, I know. I asked for it. I wrote about it last week. And I'm happy people are concerned. Really, I am.

It's just, I don't know, odd to discuss that kind of stuff. (Far different than writing about it, strangely enough.) Vasectomies aren't one of those how's-the-weather topics you feel comfortable talking about with just anyone.

For instance, I can't imagine walking up to an acquaintance at a backyard barbecue and saying, "So, how are those hemorrhoids today?"

Just can't imagine it. It's not that I don't care. It's not that I'm not concerned how his hemorrhoids are. It's just ... one of those topics. Plus, I'm trying to get to that three-bean salad over there.

And yet once people know you've had a medical procedure, any medical procedure, all bets are off, all discretion is gone. You are expected to give details, and worse, you are expected to give regular updates.

"Well, today the weather in my pants is partly painful with a 40 percent chance of swelling."

When broaching the subject, most men, I've noticed, have a punch-you-on-the-shoulder, don't-worry-you'll-be-back-in-the-game-soon attitude. They're very supportive and sympathetic. It's like I'm a soldier who took a bullet for them. "If it hadn't been you, it might have been me," their eyes say. (Or maybe it's "Better you than me, chump." It's hard to tell.)

The most sympathetic are those guys who have been there, done that. With them, suddenly, I'm in the club. It feels good. I've never been in a club before. I keep wondering when I'll get my secret password to the clubhouse. I'm picturing a rumpus room-type atmosphere where they sit around, smoke cigars and swap horror stories about their procedures like the guys did on the boat in "Jaws" about their scars.

"My doctor had cold hands."

"Oh, yeah, well, my doctor used a rusty knife."

"That's nothing, mine used a lid from a can of peas. And he had cataracts."

Women who ask me about it are completely different. Almost to a person, they have a "well-there's-another-one-taken-care-of, only-84-billion-more-to-go" tone to their voice. It's scary.

Women also don't let you get away with feeling sorry for yourself. "Oh, yeah, you think that's bad? Try squeezing a 10-pound baby out of your groin. Try being in labor for 10 hours. Try ..."

All right. I get the point. I know men can't compete when it comes to pain and discomfort in the reproductive region.

That's why women are banned from our clubhouse.

–March 17, 1999

Here's what this dad wants

I t is Father's Day. I am a father. I do not want a nice card with a joke about my expanding belly or shrinking hairline.

I want forever to see the same light in the eyes of my children - ages 7, 4 and 2 - as I see now when I pull in the driveway after work.

That is what I want.

It is Father's Day. I am a father. I do not want a necktie that lights up or glows in the dark. I do not even want a nice tie.

I want someone to assure me that my children will always be safe from harm and that their lives will be ceaselessly happy.

That is what I want.

It is Father's Day. I am a father. I do not want undercooked eggs, mushy toast or soggy cereal prepared for me by my children and delivered to me in bed. I do not even want an edible breakfast cooked by my wife.

I want to forever be as happy and as proud as when my two oldest children realized for the first time that, yes, they could ride a two-wheel bike.

That is what I want.

It is Father's Day. I am a father. I do not want to go golfing with the guys. I don't want to go bowling. I don't want to go anywhere.

I want to remember forever, even when I'm old and gray, what it was like when my children would hug me tightly around the neck each night when I leaned close to give them their goodnight kisses.

That is what I want.

It is Father's Day. I am a father. I do not want a Hawaiian shirt. I do not want a reversible belt. I do not want socks or underwear or Sansabelt slacks.

What I want is the ability to play back in my mind the sound of their giggles whenever I am low and having a bad day.

That is what I want.

It is Father's Day. I am a father. I do not want a power drill, a power sander or even a power router, whatever the heck that is.

What I want is the power to be able to follow each and every one of them all the days of their lives and protect them, guide them, comfort them. I want to do this for them, of course, but also for me, because as a father I have felt, for the first time in life, what it is like to be truly afraid and not in control. Give me the power not to fear. That is what I truly want.

It is Father's Day. I am a father. I most certainly do not want a cap that holds beer cans or a digital tire gauge or an indoor putting mat.

No. Instead give me the magical ability to instantly dry all their tears, heal their scraped knees and, someday, mend their broken hearts.

That is what I want.

It is Father's Day. I am a father. I do not want to sleep in late or spend the day in a lawn chair reading or on the couch watching a ballgame.

Call me crazy, but I want the frustrating, irritating, loud, hectic routine of life with three young, chattering, run-don't-walk children. I want this because I am smart enough to know that someday when it is gone, when I have time for myself again, I will miss it more than anything I have ever missed before.

That is what I want.

It is Father's Day. I am a father. I do not want a special dinner. I do not want a cake. I do not want to be catered to. I

do not want time to myself, I do not want time out and away.
I don't want presents or privileges or extra anything.

What I want is what I have: Three wonderful children and
a wonderful wife to raise them with me.

That is what I want.

¬June 17, 2001

It's a Mad, Mad
Mad, Mad
World

Michigan misses the dam point

The following story is true, although it may not sound like it.

About a year ago, Stephen Tvedten, a pest-control specialist who lives west of Grand Rapids, received this letter from the state:

"It has come to the attention of the Department of Environmental Quality that there has been recent unauthorized activity on (your property). You have been certified as the legal landowner and/or contractor who did the following unauthorized activity: construction and maintenance of two wood debris dams across the outlet stream of Spring Pond. A permit must be issued prior to the start of this type of activity. A review of the Department's files shows that no permits have been issued. Therefore, the Department has determined that this activity is in violation of (state law).

"The Department has been informed that one or both of the dams partially failed during a recent rain event, causing debris and flooding at downstream locations. We find that dams of this nature are inherently hazardous and cannot be permitted.

"The Department therefore orders you to cease and desist all unauthorized activities at this location, and to restore the stream to a free-flow condition by removing all wood and brush forming the dams."

The letter puzzled Tvedten. The pond in question is on a woodlot he owns near the village of Pierson, south of Big Rapids. He hadn't been there in months. And when he had been there, he certainly hadn't built any dams.

So he drove north, checked out his property, then sent the following reply to the state:

"I am the legal owner, and a couple of beavers are in the state-unauthorized process of constructing and maintaining two wood debris dams across the outlet stream of my Spring Pond. While I did not pay for, nor authorize their dam project, I think they would be highly offended that you call their skillful use of natural building materials 'debris.'

"I would like to challenge you to attempt to emulate their dam project, any dam time and/or any dam place you choose. I believe I can safely state there is no dam way that you could ever match their dam ingenuity, their dam persistence, their dam determination and/or their dam work ethic.

"If you want the dam stream restored to a dam free-flow condition, contact the dam beavers. But if you are going to arrest them (they obviously did not pay any dam attention to your dam letter, being unable to read English) be sure your read them their dam Miranda rights first. In my humble opinion, the Spring Pond beavers have a right to build their damn dams as long as the sky is blue, the grass is green and water flows downstream. They have more dam right than I to live and enjoy Spring Pond.

"In conclusion, I would like to bring to your attention a real environmental quality problem: bears are actually defecating in our woods. I definitely believe you should be persecuting the defecating bears and leave the dam beavers alone."

With his savagely witty reply, Tvedten says he was simply trying to get the state drone who wrote the letter "to laugh and admit he had made a mistake." Instead, the drone responded with a letter accusing Tvedten of illegally maintaining the dams. Tvedten responded with an angry letter, demanding to know who said so.

And that's where it stands. A year has passed with no word from the state. But Tvedten is still fuming. He'd like an apology.

"They never said they were wrong," he laments.

Of course not.

Dam bureaucrats.

– February 17, 1999

I'm totally outraged, sort of

I have decided to join with the rest of America and become deeply offended.

I base this decision on a recent article in USA Today about how just about every movie currently playing contains stereotypes that someone somewhere finds incredibly upsetting.

There's Fat Bastard, the obese Scottish character in "Austin Powers: The Spy Who Shagged Me," who threatens to sit on his enemies.

Naturally, people of weight are furious about that.

"The laziest possible trick in the humor arsenal is to trot out a fat person and laugh at him," howled Marilyn Wann, who operates a Web site called fatso.com. (No word yet from the people at bastard.com as to whether they're upset as well.)

Americans of Welsh descent are likewise ticked about the movie "Notting Hill," an otherwise inoffensive romantic comedy that includes a Welsh character who isn't very bright.

"It's a simple-minded British stereotype for a Welsh male," hissed Rees Lloyd of a Welsh legal defense fund in California. "The English have looked down their very long noses at the Welsh for a very long time."

(If I were not about to become one of the easily offended myself, I might point out to Mr. Lloyd that suggesting that all Englishmen have long noses is itself a stereotype, but I am, so I won't.)

Let's see. The American-Arab Anti-Discrimination Committee is protesting the movie "The Mummy."

"They went with the cheap laugh, comparing Arabs to camels and depicting them as smelly, disgusting, revolting womanizers," seethed the committee's Hussein Ibish.

(So far no objections from descendants of the mummy objecting to the depiction of mummies as violent and evil.)

Even "Star Wars, Episode I: The Phantom Menace" has critics.

Jews say Watto, a money-grubbing alien slaveholder, is an unflattering representation of them. The Japanese think two characters called Neimoidians make fun of them.

Even Jar Jar Binks, the annoying Gungan amphibian, has people steamed.

"Jar Jar Binks is this lisping, effeminate creature who has this whooping crying voice in times of distress," says Scott Seomin of the Gay & Lesbian Alliance Against Defamation. "He is the stereotype of a weak and emotionally unbalanced gay man."

He is? I saw the movie. Jar Jar certainly was weak and whiny, but I never got the idea that he was gay, nor do I associate those qualities with gays. I associate a fondness for the same gender with gays, and to the best of my recollection Jar Jar never asked Jim Jim for a date, so how would they know he's gay? To me he mostly looked and acted like a make-believe character in a kiddie movie.

But then I'm not very experienced at being overwrought. I'll improve.

As I mentioned, I have decided to become one with the '90s - the Golden Age of Victimization - and declare myself horrified about the stereotyping of those in my particular group. Meaning guys.

Have you ever noticed that in nearly every commercial or sitcom on television, guys are portrayed as childlike, crude, dumb, selfish or a combination of several of those traits?

Their wives and girlfriends, by comparison, spend most of their time sighing and rolling their eyes at the behavior of their male counterparts.

Clearly, Hollywood has a anti-guy bias, and as founder of the new and exceptionally shrill advocacy group GASP (Guys

Against Stereotypical Portrayals), I'm sick of it.

In the coming months, my brothers and I plan to become totally incensed and demand changes.

Just as soon as we get done scratching ourselves and drinking beer.

¬June 30, 1998

See, pigs really can fly

No matter what the commercials say, flying is hell, and it's not getting any better. Or maybe you didn't hear about the pig.

If not, allow me to make your day.

Last month, a woman named Maria Tirotta Andrews somehow convinced US Airways to let her bring her pet pig with her on a flight from Philadelphia to Seattle.

The pig, named Charlotte, slept for most of the trip but went nuts as the plane began its descent and - I'm sorry, I simply can't say it any better than the news report - "started squealing, tried to get into the cockpit and charged through the cabin discharging feces as it went."

That's actually not the unusual part. Ask a flight attendant. The same sort of behavior takes place on return flights from Cancun all the time.

No, here are the really good parts of this story:

1) Charlotte is not one of those trendy little pygmy pigs that people bought as pets several years ago. She weighs 300 pounds. I can just imagine the flight attendant greeting passengers as they board - "Hi, hello, how are you?" - and here comes a 300-pound pork chop. What do you say, "Enjoy your flight, Mr. Ziffel"? You just know that after the pig passed, one of them whispered to the other, "Uh, better order more peanuts."

2) Andrews got Charlotte on the plane by telling the airline

she needed the pig with her because of a heart condition (hers, not the pig's). At first I thought, "What's the pig going to do, give her CPR?" ("Breathe, dammit, oink!")

Then I learned that Andrews is exceptionally close to the pig (apparently there are no singles bars in Philadelphia) and needed the pig to calm her nerves. She even got a note from her doctor. That I'd like to see: "Dear Airline People, please allow my patient to take a 300-pound incontinent pig on the airplane with her. Thank you. Oh, and whatever you do, don't serve BLTs."

What's even weirder is that the airline bought it. They granted Charlotte "service animal" status, which basically means Charlotte was deemed this woman's seeing-eye swine. Better still, apparently no one at the airline bothered to ask whether Charlotte was a small Charlotte's Web-sized pig or a pig the size of Delaware.

That's one airline I have GOT to fly.

The ones I fly on now have all these, you know, rules and stuff. Return your seat to the upright position. Buckle your seat belt. No smoking. Call your mother. It's a hassle. And yet here is an airline where, clearly, anything goes. One carry-on bag? To heck with that, I'm bringing my house with me. And maybe a masseuse. And a cappuccino machine. (Hope that sucking sound doesn't disturb the pilot.)

And you know, I've always enjoyed the calming effects of my aquarium. Think I'll bring it along next time, plug it into one of the computer ports. Then I'm going up front to take a crack at flying this puppy. Whee-heee! Say, what's that red button over there do?

I hope this one little incident with the pig and the feces and the screaming hysterical passengers doesn't discourage US Airways from continuing this anything-goes policy. I'll fly with you guys any time, pig or no pig.

Just don't seat me next to one. I like having the armrest, and you know some pigs: They can be such hogs.

–November 22, 2000

John Glenn blasts off once again

There I was, in my basement, twisting dials on my short wave radio with little success.

Skreee-raw-shhhhhhhh. Squonk-hrrrrr-ssssssss.

When all of a sudden I picked up this:

"Mission Control, this is space shuttle Discovery. Do you copy?"

"This is Mission Control in Houston. Go ahead, Discovery."

"He's got another complaint."

"Oh for the love of ... what is it this time?"

"He forgot to pack his Metamucil. Says if he doesn't get it he'll get - and we quote - 'bound up tighter'na overwound Timex.'"

"A what?"

"I don't know. He's got all these weird expressions for things. He called the captain a whippersnapper yesterday."

"Well, tell him that no one winds watches anymore and no one buys
Timexes."

"We did."

"And?"

"He called us young punks and said HIS Timex winds, and it's 'taken a licking and kept on ticking' for 35 years now."

"It's done what?"

"Unknown, Mission Control. He's full of stuff like that."

"Did you tell him it's a little odd to lick a watch, much less keep one for 35 years?"

"Affirmative. Says he keeps everything. Old watches, toilet paper tubes, string. We caught him saving the used stroganoff tubes the other day."

"Stroganoff tubes?"

"Says we'd do it, too, if we'd lived through the Depression."

"Uh, hold on a second, Discovery. We show a malfunction in the port side directional indicator."

"The left turn signal? That's Glenn again. Keeps flicking it on and forgetting to turn it off. We traveled 400,000 miles the last time before we caught it."

"Did you mention it to him?"

"Affirmative."

"And?"

"He said that in his day they didn't need fancy-schmancy gadgets. Says if they needed to signal a turn they'd just stick an arm out the window."

"But that's absurd. You can't open windows in space."

"We know, Houston."

"Well, what does he say?"

"He says that in his day they didn't NEED windows. And then he launched into a 45-minute story about the old Apollo missions."

"What's wrong with that?"

"It was the 22nd time he told it."

"At least the old man's memory is still working."

"Uh, not really, Mission Control. He keeps forgetting we're in space. He tried to go for a walk around the block yesterday."

"Any other problems, Discovery?"

"Well, he keeps insisting on a senior citizen discount at dinner. And he wants to eat at 4."

"Yes. We were afraid that might happen."

"And he's constantly griping about the cold."

"So turn up the heat."

"We did."

"And?"

"He says, 'What are you punks trying to do, roast me?'"

"Sounds bad."

"It is, Houston. The navigator is threatening to cut his tether on the space walk if he brings up his damned prostate one more time."

"Understandable, Discovery. Anything else?"

"Depends."

"Depends on what, Discovery?"

"No, we mean he also says he forgot his Depends."

"I'm afraid we can't do much about that, Discovery. You're 1,000 miles above the Earth."

"Uh, then, Houston, I think we might have a problem."

"How so?"

"The rest of the crew wants to come home NOW."

–November 11, 1998

In a weird galaxy, far, far away

Sure, I could have taken out a second mortgage and stood in line for two weeks with a bunch of ripening geeks in Yoda masks to get tickets to see "Star Wars: Episode I - The Phantom Menace."

But I didn't because I already know what happens.

SCENE ONE:

Obi-Wan Kenobi (Ewan McGregor): "Hello, my name is Obi-Wan. You may have noticed that I look nothing like Sir Alec Guinness, who will play me in the future, but at least I have a British accent. Please, Jedi Master, can you teach me the ways of The Force?"

Qui-Gon Jinn (Liam Neeson): "Of course I will, young Obi-Wan. I will teach you the ways of The Force, even though I, a great actor, feel a bit ridiculous wearing this stupid cape and Jesus beard in a kiddie flick after all of the sophisticated roles I have played over the course of my long and illustrious career."

Obi-Wan Kenobi: "What?"

Qui-Gon Jinn: "Never mind. Listen, when you are able to snatch this pebble from my palm, you will have learned the ways of The Force."

Obi-Wan Kenobi: "Um, Jedi Master, wrong gimmick. I think that's the opening for the television show 'Kung Fu.'"

Qui-Gon Jinn: "Ah, so it is. Perhaps, then, we should duel with light sabers! En garde!"

Obi-Wan Kenobi: "Light sabers? Are you nuts? Why should I use a stupid sword when I have this laser gun?"

Qui-Gon Jinn: "I have always wondered that myself, Obi-Wan. You have powers far beyond your acting ability. Perhaps it is time we went on a secret mission."

SCENE TWO:

Qui-Gon Jinn: "Well, here we are on the planet Naboo."

Obi-Wan Kenobi: "Naboo? That's the corniest name for a planet I've ever heard. George Lucas has had 15 years to write this prequel, and that's the best he could come up with?"

Qui-Gon Jinn: "Apparently so, my brash young apprentice. Oh, look, here comes the beautiful teen queen of Naboo."

Obi-Wan Kenobi: "Hubba hubba!"

Qui-Gon Jinn: "Hush, young one. Don't be so impolite."

Obi-Wan Kenobi: "But hubba hubba is Naboobian for 'Hiya, queenie.'"

Qui-Gon Jinn: "Oh."

Queen Amidala (Natalie Portman): "Would you two stop babbling? I need your help. A greedy, expansionistic business cartel wants to take over my planet."

Qui-Gon Jinn: "My god! Quick, tell us the name of this evil cartel and its leader!"

Queen Amidala: "Microsoft, led by the evil Darth Gates."

Qui-Gon Jinn: "Horrors! We have no choice but to advance the plot by taking you to the planet of Tatooine to encounter young Anakin Skywalker!"

Obi-Wan and Queen Amidala (in unison): "Who?"

Qui-Gon Jinn: "Good grief, people, don't you read scripts?"

SCENE THREE

Qui-Gon Jinn: "Well, here we are. Look, there is young Anakin right there."

Queen Amidala: "A very handsome boy. He will certainly make a fine poseable action figure retailing for $8.99 at a Toys R Us near you."

Qui-Gon Jinn: "How right you are. That is why we must rescue him from his slave master, the evil Watto."

Obi-Wan Kenobi: "Watto? You mean that elephant over there?"

Qui-Gon Jinn: "Hush, young one. He is very sensitive about his nose. If he hears you, he will challenge one of us to a race on those flying motorcycle things, winner take

Skywalker. And I get motion-sick."

Watto: "I challenge one of you to a race on those flying motorcycle things, winner take Skywalker!"

Qui-Gon Jinn: "See? I told you so."

TO BE CONTINUED ... or maybe not.

–May 15, 1999

The way they do weather is snow good

Good evening and welcome to the 6 o'clock Action News, I'm Bill Fulluvit. In Washington D.C. tonight, President Bill Clinton lingers near death due to acute food poisoning. And a major outbreak of mad cow disease has killed half of Great Britain. But first, we begin with comprehensive team coverage of the snow storm of this or any other century. It's going to be a big one, Joan."

CO-ANCHOR: "That's right, Bill. And that's why we've come up with a ridiculously dramatic logo and drum intensive music for our coverage. We call it (drums, logo flashing) Blizzard 2000. Let's go live to our Doppler radar center, which is in actuality just 12 feet away from where I sit now. Doug?"

WEATHERGUY: "Thanks, Joan. As you can clearly see on our exclusive "Action News At 6 Super-Duper Much Better Than The Other Station's Doppler Radar," a high pressure pattern of intense snow activity is building to the west."

CO-ANCHOR: "But Doug, that appears to be eight states away."

WEATHERGUY: "That's right, Joan. Only eight states away. That's why we're suggesting that every school district within the sound of my voice immediately cancel school for at least the next week, if not longer."

CO-ANCHOR: "Whew. Thank you, Doug. When do you expect Blizzard 2000 to hit?"

WEATHERGUY: "It's hard to say, Joan. Could be today.

Could be next week. Could be never. Weather's kind of funny that way."

CO-ANCHOR (putting on concerned face No. 3): "How much snow are we talking about, Doug?"

WEATHERGUY: "Again, Joan, it's tough to say. Could be an inch, could be 10 inches. Weather systems are inherently unpredictable."

CO-ANCHOR: "So are you saying that we might be needlessly and purposely hyping this snow as a way to attract viewership in a sweeps month period, during which our station sets its advertising rates, thus determining future revenue?"

WEATHERGUY: "No, Joan, what I'm saying is that everyone within the sound of my voice, including heart surgeons, should immediately drop what they're doing and rush to the store for emergency supplies just in case."

CO-ANCHOR: "Thank goodness for modern technology, Doug. And thank you for that incredibly worrisome report."

ANCHOR: "Let's switch now to preternaturally blonde reporter Melissa Perky at the airport. Melissa?"

PERKY: "Thanks, Bill. As you can see, I'm standing here freezing my tuckus off outside of the airport for no apparent reason, since the skies are clear and there's no snow falling. Airport officials tell me, though, that they may cancel flights if and when the snow comes, but probably not."

ANCHOR: "Hmm. The situation does in fact appear as if it could conceivably at some indeterminate point in the future become grim. Very grim. How are passengers holding up?"

PERKY: "Pretty well, Bill. In fact, they're acting pretty much as if nothing is going on. Which it isn't."

ANCHOR: "Fascinating. Thank you, Melissa. Let's switch now to reporter Allen Smiley, who is standing by at an Ace Hardware store. Allen, are people buying shovels and snowblowers?"

SMILEY: "Yes, they are, Bill. As the owner of the store told me, 'Of course they're buying that stuff. It's winter, you dummy.'"

– February 21, 2000

Bad ideas worth a lot in Hollywood

Today's lesson: How to become a rich and famous Hollywood screenwriter.

Step 1: Buy a TV.

Step 2: Watch it.

Step 3: Write a screenplay based on what you see.

And there you have it. You are now officially on the road to being a rich, famous Hollywood screenwriter. That'll be a thousand dollars, please.

What's that? You don't know which television show to base your screenplay on?

C'mon, bunky, you're not trying. Or at the very least you're not attending your local Cineplex very often. If you were, you'd know that the pick-a-show-any-show trend is in full flower.

The past few years have seen movies based on "Shaft," "The Beverly Hillbillies," "The Flintstones," "Charlie's Angels," "Mission: Impossible" and more.

Each and every one of those movies - pardon me for this term, but it's the only one that truly fits - sucked. But that hardly matters to you, the aspiring screenplay writer.

Your only concern: Pick a TV show - no matter how banal, no matter how painfully stupid - that reminds members of my generation (the baby boomers) of our distant youth, take 15 minutes or so and type a screenplay loosely based on it (spelling and grammar skills optional), send it in to a studio, then sit back and wait for your check.

Sounds easy, right? That's because it is! That's the beauty of this scheme. Hollywood used to require that screenplays have some depth to them. Dramas were supposed to be dramatic. Action films were supposed to be somewhat believable. Comedies - this one will astound you - actually were supposed to be funny. These things took ability, sweat, time. Now all you need is Nick at Nite.

Watch for a couple of hours, find a show that hasn't been pile-driven into the ground already by the movie studios, bang out a script, then practice your Scrooge McDuck dive into piles of money.

You don't believe me? Your honor, I would like to enter into evidence the newest theaterical release, "Josie and the Pussycats."

If there was ever a TV show that would cause you say, "There's no WAY they could ever turn that into a live action film for adults," it would be "Josie and the Pussycats."

Obscure ain't the word for the show it's based on. It was a short-lived, utterly unremarkable, barely memorable, badly animated cartoon back in the '70s about an all-girl rock band that wore costumes reminiscent of Playboy bunnies.

The Pussycats (the wink-wink, nudge-nudge name was no doubt some clever TV writer's idea of a joke: tee hee, I snuck a double entendre into a wholesome kiddie show!) were, if I'm not mistaken, a spinoff from another cartoon, "The Archies," which was based on the comic book.

So that's where Hollywood is these days in terms of creativity. They're now doing bad live action films aimed at adults based on bad kiddie shows that were themselves spun off of bad kiddie shows that were based on bad comic books. That loud thumping you hear is Alfred Hitchcock rolling over in his grave.

Don't worry. He'll roll back over again.

I hear they're doing a movie version of "Hogan's Heroes."

–April 16, 2001

Here's how to get on 'Springer'

I went and applied for a spot on "The Jerry Springer Show." It seemed like the '90s thing to do.

"So what makes you think you're Springer material?" said Miss Snodgrass, the show's producer. "We have high standards, you know."

"Well, I'm the product of a forbidden love affair between my mother and Big Foot," I said. "That's why I have all this hair on my back."

"That's good," said Miss Snodgrass, "but not good enough anymore, I'm afraid."

"Well," I said, "I've also had a 36-year infatuation with my mother's sister's nephew."

"But wouldn't your mother's sister's nephew be you?"

"Plus, I was abducted by aliens for purposes of diabolical medical experimentation."

"Really?"

"They gave me back, though, when I complained that their doctor wasn't on my insurance plan."

Miss Snodgrass frowned and said: "That's all well and good. But tell me, how's your left cross?"

"My left what?"

"And your jab. How's your jab? You have to have a good jab to get on the Springer show these days."

"A jab?" I said. "You mean as in a punch?"

"Of course, silly. It's our new schtick."

"Your new schtick?"

"Sure. It used to be we could hook viewers with topics like `I Was A Vegetarian Vampire' or `My Sister Slept With Your Sister - And Now She Wants Her Money Back!' Or even `My Husband Pollinated My Garden Club - So I Pruned Him.' "

"Sounds like must-see TV."

"It was. For awhile. But plain old dysfunction doesn't cut it anymore."

"It doesn't?"

"No sirree. We discovered we were losing viewers to Saint Oprah and her goody-two shoes act."

"Perish the thought."

"Indeed. Can you imagine people preferring a conversation about - ugh - books to a show about `I Slept With A Gorilla And Now I Feel Like a Monkey'? Or the classic `I Married My Siamese Twin, But Now We're Separated.' "

"What's this country coming to?"

"Tell me about it. We were about to go under. Then Jerry said, `Remember how much fun it was when the male transvestite lesbians got into a fight over who was more Ellen's type? Why don't we do that everyday?' " And that's exactly what we did."

"You mean people get into fistfights every day?"

"Don't be silly," she said. "Sometimes they throw chairs or gouge eyes instead. It's wonderful TV. The more fighting the better. These days, a guest says a word or two, then it's biff, bam, boom!"

"Sounds like the World Wrestling Federation."

"Exactly! Except some of our guests have better moves."

"And people are tuning in for this?"

"Tuning in? Ratings are through the roof! People can't get enough. Especially the kids."

"Kids watch your show?"

"Sure. When they get home from school. We consider it educational TV."

"Educational TV?"

"Sure. We teach them conflict resolution."

"Whomping on one another is conflict resolution?"

"On our show it is," she said. "So, tell me, how are you at giving atomic wedgies?"

"Not very good, I'm afraid," I said. "In fact, I'm a

milquetoast when it comes to fighting. I've never been in a fight in my life."

"Great! We'll put you on next Tuesday's show."

"Really?"

"Sure. You know how hard it is to find human punching bags these days?"

–March 15, 1998

Yearbooks don't show the true high school

A student e-mailed me and asked if I could convince my newspaper to help the class of 1999 at Mt. Morris High School publish a new yearbook.

In case you missed it, the school's computers, for the second year in a row, ate the graduating class' yearbook. (What, no dogs in Mt. Morris?)

That's sad, of course. And I wrote back to this student saying, sure, I'd help if I could, even though in truth there is probably little I or the newspaper can do, aside from providing a few old photos and stories.

But what I didn't say is that I bet there are more than a few students who secretly aren't upset at all about the yearbook going down the cybertoilet.

They're the ones who, odds are, wouldn't have been in there very much anyway.

The geeks.

The freaks.

The stoners.

The loners.

The quiet.

The chess clubbers.

The painfully skinny.

The painfully fat.

The brains.

The Future Farmers of America.

The ones who take marching band a little too seriously.

The shop class guys.

The ones who think getting blotto drunk at a party is not only stupid and dangerous, but dull.

The ones who think rap songs about murder and rape aren't entertaining.

The wallflowers.

The out of step.

The ugly.

The not-yet-blossomed.

The shy.

The acned.

In other words, the vast majority of the student body.

Every yearbook I've ever seen concentrates 80 percent of its space (aside from those stiff, primped portraits) on 20 percent of its students. That's not a judgment. That's just how it is.

Yearbooks are a chronicle of early bloomers, those students who early on learn the steps to the dance of popularity.

Cheerleaders.

Jocks.

The zany.

The loud look-at-mes.

The good-looking.

The charismatic.

The mega-partiers.

The class president (who, guaranteed, fits one or more of the above categories).

If you looked at most yearbooks, you would think there were 20 people in most graduating classes.

If yearbooks are supposed to be a travelogue of high school life, they fail miserably, through no fault of the yearbook staff.

Yearbook photographers and the editors who select the photos that make the cut are, after all, students, too. If you were them, would you run another photo of the charming, handsome class president getting a whipped cream pie in the face from a popular teacher at a pep assembly? Or would you run a boring black and white of the shy, bespectacled girl in sewing class who is so quiet you suspect she has no vocal cords?

You know which one you'd run. That's human nature,

especially as it is practiced on the high school level. But it misses the fact that for many kids, high school is not some happy-go-lucky lark out of an Archie comic book.

It's a painful journey best forgotten altogether or learned from, then forgotten.

For these students, a yearbook, if they bought one at all, would only be a reminder trailing them throughout their lives of the not-quite-ready-for-prime-time people they once were and would just as soon leave behind.

–January 19, 2000

President Bush has lessons to share

I f I were President Bush, I'd take the Oval Office phone off the hook, tell my secretary to keep the problems of the nation and the world at the door, then I'd sit down and pen a letter to my daughter.

It would go something like this.

Dear Jenna: First of all, I love you. I wanted to say that first because you won't like what I'm going to say next.

Sweetie, you have a drinking problem.

And by problem, I don't mean that I think you're an alcoholic. I doubt that you are. Yet. But the signs are that you could be on your way. And even if you're not on your way to alcoholism, you sure as shootin' could be on your way to some really big problems that go along with "normal" college drinking - date rape, dying in a car crash, a crippled reputation and the like.

I know, I know, you're rolling your eyes, right? But, honey, sometimes it's easier for others to see patterns in your life than it is for you to see them, especially when you're just 19 and don't know the ways of the world yet.

In you, I see a pattern beginning. And as your dad, it scares me.

A month ago, you were ticketed for drinking beer in a nightclub. You had to appear in court, where the judge ordered you to go to alcohol-awareness class and do public service.

At the time, your mother and I thought - just like everyone else - well, kids will be kids. Plus, you have all the pressures of being "the president's kid." So it was somewhat understandable.

Then last week, just a month after your first encounter, you were ticketed again for trying to buy booze at a restaurant in Austin with a fake ID.

That tells me a few things, honey. It tells me that you didn't take the first offense seriously at all. Maybe you went to your alcohol classes and did your public service, but clearly none of it sank in.

I know, I know. You're thinking, "Everyone drinks in college. It's no big deal. You're just another boring, over-reacting adult."

True, but I'm also an adult who's been there. I spent four years in college, and that's WHY I'm a boring, overreactive adult.

See, I had what you might call a real good time. I was the life of party at a lot of parties at Yale. And at the time, and for years afterward, I thought, "Man, those were the days."

But, hon, I paid for those good times. I know it's impossible for you to understand at your age, but things have a way of coming back on you.

Look at me. I continued drinking all through my 20s and 30s. I was still the life of the party. But I also got arrested for driving drunk when I was 30. I never told you and your sister because I was ashamed and didn't want you think bad things about your old man.

I quit drinking altogether when I was 40, in part because I didn't want to set a poor example for you kids, but also because I was starting to realize that for decades people hadn't been taking me seriously because they thought of me as just good ol' party-time George.

I still suffer from it. Even during the election, people had questions about me. I'm sure some people still wonder whether I'll turn to the bottle when the pressure is on.

I won't, of course. I licked those demons years ago. But that's just one of the prices you pay for a life of drinking, and I see a lot of myself in you, sweetheart. I see the sins of the father revisiting the daughter. I don't want that for you. You're my sweet Texas rose.

Be smarter than your old man, eh? Quit now.
Love, Dad.

¬*June 4, 2001*

The poll says: Polls are useless

Al Gore is beaming this week because the latest polls show he has pulled into a dead heat with George W. Bush after trailing by as many as 15 points.

But did he really?

Well, no. A presidential election isn't a football game. There's no score, no touchdowns, not even any endzone dances, so in actuality Gore and Bush have been in a dead heat all along and will be until after the voting booths close on Nov. 7.

Polls are imaginary, and yet everyone pretends that they're not. We read story after story about how Candidate A is trailing or Candidate B is surging or how Candidate A says he doesn't believe in polls. (Of course any candidate who says he doesn't believe in polls is always the one the polls say is behind.) But we seldom stop to question how stupid and unreal and counterproductive polls are.

An example: After the Republican convention, Bush was said to be way ahead of Gore. Some polls had him as a 15-point favorite, which is close to landslide territory.

But then, glory be, after the Democratic convention, Gore was said to have made an amazing "comeback." He, too, "surged" and "pulled even," and now the pollsters are predicting a close race right to the end.

That's amazing, especially when you consider that political pollsters routinely boast that their polls are "scientific" and accurate to within 4 percentage points.

So were the pollsters merely wrong after the Republican convention, or are Americans truly that fickle? Did a full 11 to 15 percent of all voting Americans suddenly switch their allegiance from Bush or undecided to Gore after the Democratic convention?

It would seem so. But how could that be when the nightly news reminded us nightly that hardly anyone was actually watching the convention? How could Gore get that much "bounce" when most nights of the convention drew fewer viewers than the "Facts of Life" rerun where Tootie loses her retainer?

The answer is he can't and he didn't.

Polls typically question 600 or so voters and from that they say they are able to tell how the rest of us will vote. It's all mathematical and scientific and there's no chance they are wrong, as any pollster will tell you. But think about it: How do most of us react when we get a call at home from somebody selling a product or conducting a poll?

I don't know about you, but last week I picked up the phone and there was that pause after I said hello and I knew it was yet another call from VISA (they're obsessed with me) and a young man asked if Andrew Heller was at home.

I said, "Yes, but he's too busy pruning the dandelions that grow from his ears to come to the phone. But the King of Sweden is here. Would you like to speak with him?" And then I hung up. I think a lot of people, sick of people bugging them at home, do that sort of thing.

So how do the pollsters know people aren't yanking their chains? How do they know that 43 percent of the people who say they are voting for Gore only said so to be funny?

The answer is they don't. All they know for sure is what a relative few people say they feel at the point they were asked. And yet the pollsters continue to release their results as if they're the gospel, and I think the end result is that many people wind up voting the way the polls tell them other people are voting.

A radical theory? Nah. And the polls say three out four Americans agree with me.

Would I lie?

–September 5, 2000

Value of debates is debatable

The problem with presidential debates is they rarely tell us anything that we don't already know.

Please tell me that you don't tune in to hear what the candidates think on the issues. You should already know that, at least in a general sense. They're called news stories, people. Try them, you'll like them.

I suspect most of us watch in order to "be there" in case one of the candidates implodes. We want to see it if George Dubbya goes postal and calls Gore a "major league donkey-portal." We want to see if Al Gore's gears and switches freeze up from the artificial perspiration secreted by the cyber-glands in his forehead.

Alas, candidates these days are so well coached, rehearsed and programmed that we rarely get a feel for their true characters.

Me, I crave a look at the men behind the curtain. I want to cut down the tree and count the rings, see the evidence of the fires and storms and calm seasons that shaped its growth. I want to see if these men have a sense of humor, and if so, is it an odd one? I want to know if they have souls - if they've ever held a rock and just looked at it, if they've ever spent an hour lying on the grass under a tree looking up at the canopy of leaves above them. Heck, I want to know if they've ever accidentally belched in a crowded elevator or whether they cried when their children were born.

We need a new debate format. I say we hook them up to

polygraphs and ask them the following:

Paper or plastic?

What did you dress up as for Halloween when you were a kid?

What are your views on Jet-Skis and snowmobiles? Obnoxious, nature-disturbing horrors or yeeha-fun?

What is Matchbox 20? Who are the Dixie Chicks?

Do you hold doors for ladies? Have you always?

What's the one food you secretly love that might embarrass you?

What was your nickname in sixth grade? (If they didn't have one, then I'm not voting for them.)

Have you ever changed a diaper? How about when the kid had diarrhea?

Betty or Veronica? MaryAnn or Ginger? (If they answer "Who?" then I'm not voting for them, either.)

What celebrity or political big-wig smells the worst?

Do you ever worry about being assassinated?

If you're wrong in a fight with your wife, do you admit it? Ever ask for directions?

When you go to political fund-raisers, do you ever feel like screaming, I hate each and every one of you!"

Why do you really do what you do? And don't forget, you're attached to a lie detector.

Ever steal anything as a kid?

Who is the most qualified person for the presidency in the United States today? Not the most electable, but the most qualified.

What do you really think of your opponent?

Do you like dirty jokes? Polish jokes? Gay jokes? Do you repeat them?

Is there an afterlife or is this it? Again, don't forget the polygraph.

Who do you hate the most in the whole entire world and why? Ever litter?

Have you ever come close, at least in your mind, to divorcing your current wife? If so, what were the reasons?

In private, when angered, are you a yeller?

That's what I would ask. And the first one who interrupted an answer by the other would disappear through a trap door.

–October 8, 2000

Lemonade is a liability

Mommy?"

"Yes, dear?"

"I want to open a lemonade stand."

"Oh, my."

"What's wrong, mommy?"

"Well, dear, it's just that opening a lemonade stand is a very serious undertaking."

"It is?"

"Oh, yes. For instance, what will you use for start-up costs?"

"Start-up what?"

"Start-up costs. You know, to buy lemons and sugar."

"I could use my piggy bank."

"That's fine, dear, but remember we agreed on a substantial penalty for early withdrawal of any and all piggy bank funds."

"Yes, mommy."

"And then, of course, there's liability insurance."

"Lia what?"

"Liability, dear. You know, in case someone sues you."

"Why would anyone sue me, mommy?"

"Why is the sky blue, son."

"Huh?"

"Look, you could be sued for lots of reasons. Someone could choke on an ice cube or turn green from a lemon allergy."

"Golly!"

"And if they sue you and you don't have insurance you could lose all of your assets."

"My what?"

"Your bike, dear. They'd take your bike."

"Gosh!"

"Now, are you ready for the inspectors?"

"The what?"

"The inspectors, dear. They make sure you're up to code."

"What's code, mommy?"

"No one's quite sure, dear. But in your case, the health inspector will probably check to make sure your food-handling equipment is sterile."

"My what?"

"Your hands, dear. He'll want to make sure you wash your hands. Plus, he'll check to see you have adequate bathroom facilities, refrigeration units and a dishwasher with an anti-bacterial temperature gauge."

"Wow."

"And the building inspector will want to see that your stand is properly zoned and constructed, and that you have an adequate sprinkler system."

"A sprinkler system? For a lemonade stand?"

"Fire safety standards. Incidentally, were you planning to use union labor to build your stand?"

"Uh, no. I was going to build it myself."

"Tsk. Then you'll need security, I'm afraid."

"Security?"

"For when the union picketers show up."

"Oh, boy."

"And do you plan to run this operation by yourself?"

"No, Bobby's going to help."

"I see. Well, that means you'll need a payroll system." "But I was just going to let Bobby drink free lemonade."

"Sorry, dear, that simply won't do. How would you be able to withhold taxes?"

"Taxes?"

"Of course. There's city, state, federal taxes, plus FICA."

"What's FICA?"

"No one's sure, dear, but it means the government gets a lot of your money."

"Gee."

"And of course yours will be an equal opportunity lemonade stand, right?"

"Huh?"

"That means you'll serve anyone who's thirsty."

"Sure, except for Susie. She's just a dumb old girl."

"Mmm. I'm afraid the National Organization for Women won't stand for that kind of sexist discrimination, young man. And may I add that the term 'girl' is insulting and derogatory. Susie is a "developing womyn."

"She is? Gosh, mommy, I had no idea."

"Well, now you do. So, is there anything I can do to help with your lemonade stand?"

"I don't think I want one anymore, mommy."

"What are you going to do instead, dear?"

"Watch TV. It's seems a whole lot easier."

¬June 25, 1995

My obsession comes to a chicken head

The chicken head lives in my consciousness and will not leave.

I see it when I wake in the morning. I see it at lunch. I see it at dinner. It haunts my dreams. It's dead, but it lives.

Leave me alone, chicken head!

The chicken head welded itself to my brain pan last week when I saw a photo of it in a newspaper.

It was deep-fried and golden-brown, but it still looked like a chicken head - beak, comb, a slight, almost wry expression on it's finger-lickin' good face that seemed to say, "Momma told me there'd be days like this."

A woman in Virginia found it in a box of chicken wings from McDonald's. She screamed when she saw it, of course. Wouldn't you? Then she did what most Americans do when something bad happens to them - she called a TV station.

Maybe it was a hoax. Maybe she just wants to sue. Maybe it never happened. To me, it doesn't matter. The damage has been done. I have not been the same since.

I will admit it. I am squeamish about food. I once ate a chicken nugget with a tiny marble of gristle in it. I've never eaten another one since. And I have repeated the story so often that the term "chicken knuckle" has become part of my family's lexicon.

There was a story circulating around my hometown a few

years ago about a pizzeria that had something, um, extra in the sauce, put there by a prankster employee. (Phone me and I'll tell you.)

The story couldn't possibly be true. Just couldn't. The mind rebels at the mere thought of it happening on this or any other plane of existence.

But still I haven't eaten there since. And I probably never will again.

My brother Dan was once in hotel-restaurant management. He told me, "Don't ever send back food in a restaurant. Ever."

I asked why and he said, "Just. Don't."

I haven't. I could get a steak with hooves and hair still attached and I'd smile and eat my salad.

I mean, who knows who works back there? Jeffrey Dahmer worked somewhere once. Beavis & Butt-head were presumably based on real people. Who knows what evil lurks in the hearts and minds of those who put food in front of my face?

Life is one long leap of faith. I realize that. If we had no faith in our fellow men and women, it would be impossible to get out of bed in the morning for fear of what might happen.

That's why I've tried to smile when my Journal co-workers have joked about the chicken head.

"Hey, parts is parts," one said.

"It probably tasted better than the wings," said another colleague.

Someone else said they didn't know that McDonald's served chicken McNoggins.

I've even tried to look on the bright side of things. At least this seems to suggest that McDonald's uses chicken in its products. (Have you ever looked inside a McNugget? Don't.)

But my mind keeps returning to that face, that horrible, deep-fried, golden-brown face.

May it leave me someday.

–December 6, 2000

Thongs for the memories

You wanna hear something wild?" asked a friend of mine.

We were sitting at a bar shortly after Valentine's Day. I figured he meant he had a good dirty joke for me.

"Sure," I said. "Is this the one with the chickens and the traveling egg salesman?"

"No," he said, lowering his voice and leaning in toward me. "My wife gave me thong underwear for Valentine's Day."

"How's she look in them?" I asked.

"No, you don't understand. She gave them to me. To wear. And I am."

"Am what?" I said, my eyes narrowing.

"Wearing them. Right now. And you know what, I gotta admit, I actually like 'em."

Oh, Lord. I knew it was going to come to this. The feminization of the American male is nearing completion.

It began way back in the late 1950s when a pair of women in a Greenwich Village bar convinced their dates to fast-dance with them. All of the women in the bar that night decided it was so cute and wonderful that they pestered their boyfriends and husbands to fast- dance, too. And from there, it was only a matter of time before women coast to coast had convinced men to fast-dance or else.

This led to other barriers falling. Hair, for instance. It used to be the height of froofiness for a guy to have long hair. The '60s ended that, of course.

Then came jewelry. A man who wore necklaces and bracelets back when I was growing up would have been considered highly suspect, which is why you never saw anyone do it.

Then came Mr. T. And the next thing you know, men everywhere were wearing more jewelry than Elizabeth Taylor, fast-dancing at the disco and ordering blue drinks at the bar.

In recent years, men have started wearing earrings as well, which is just plain weird. I've never considered myself much of a he-man, but I did grow up identifying with he-man types like John Wayne.

Correct me if I'm wrong, but I don't think John Wayne ever wore an earring. If he did, the other cowpokes would have laughed him out of the saloon.

I even saw unisex perfume the other day. I know cologne and perfume are basically the same thing, still any guy who wears unisex perfume probably cuts the crust off his toast, too, if you know what I mean.

And now it's the underwear. You could see this one coming. Way back when, there were two kinds of men's underwear - boxers and briefs. Then came Mark Spitz and his Speedos. And for lack of any evidence that says otherwise, I'm calling that the beginning of the end. Suddenly, you couldn't go to the pool without some guy (and always a guy who shouldn't) Speedoing out all over the place.

Speedos opened the door to bikini underwear. And bikini underwear led, inevitably, to thongs, which I understand are quite the hot item among young men because they - I can hardly write this without gagging - don't leave visible panty lines.

I'm sorry, this is just not right. There are supposed to be some differences between men and women. There just are.

I said this to my friend, and he said, "Don't be so old-fashioned. Listen, you ought to try a pair. They're really comfortable."

Comfortable? I doubt that. The last time I had underwear shoved up in thong territory was back in junior high when some guys in the locker room gave me a wedgie. I don't recall it being "comfortable." I recall it made me walk funny for the rest of the day.

So, no. No thong underwear for me. Someone's got to make a stand.

I'm sure The Duke would be proud of me.

–February 19, 2001

Moon
& Friends

Keeping promises a scary prospect

I asked Moon Dimple, my boyhood pal and self-appointed Finger On the Pulse of America, usually the middle one, what he thought of the big Promise Keepers rally in Washington last weekend.

"Not much," he said. "The feminists were right. Those guys should've stayed home where they belong."

Moon agreeing with feminists on anything is an unusual thing, indeed. Back in college, he made NOW's "Most-Wanted Oinkers" list for suggesting a campus policy requiring coeds to wear miniskirts at all times, regardless of the weather.

Plus, he still audaciously refuses to call a manhole cover a "personnel access portal."

So I asked him to explain his objection to the rally: "I mean, 500,000 guys, all praying and weeping for the courage to go home and tell their wives that they intend to be the boss from here on out. Sounds right up your alley."

"Sorry, in my alley we don't weep," he replied. "Nor do we carry on, flail our arms, moan, hug or beat drums. In my alley, we keep our feelings to ourselves and the only time we hug another guy is after a particularly important touchdown, and even then we're embarrassed about it afterward."

"But I think that was, in part, the point of the rally," I said. "To break with traditional patterns of male behavior."

"Yeah, but only some patterns. You notice that? They get out there in Washington and cry and discuss their feelings and mope about their shortcomings as husbands and fathers, which is definitely nontraditional behavior as far as guys go. Then they turn around and say, 'So, I guess the only solution is to go home and tell my wife to submit to my leadership.' Which is about as traditional as you can get, am I right?"

"Well, yes," I said. "But I would think you'd be happy about that. Aren't you the one who's always saying you wear the pants in your family?"

"Yeah, I say that," he said. "But not when my wife can hear."

"Ho ho," I said. "So this macho thing is just talk with you, then."

"No. I believe what I believe. But I also have to live in the real world, and in the real world my wife would kill me if I said I was the boss."

"Maybe you should have gone to the rally, then. At least they had the courage to tell their women they were taking charge."

"Yeah, but you'll notice they said it when they were several hundred to several thousand miles away from their wives. When they get home, how many of them are going to have the guts to walk up to their wives and say, 'From now on, honey, I'm in charge.'"

"I don't know," I said.

"Well, I do: None. Not if they want sex again this century, anyway. That's called traditional female behavior."

I had to admit he was right. Still, that didn't explain his opposition to Promise Keepers, I said. What's so bad about an organization that encourages men to keep their promises?

"Nothing," he said. "Some guys ARE jerks about the big stuff. They spend too much time at the bar. They can't remember their kids' names. The only time they talk to their wives is to ask for a beer. Those guys should keep their promises."

"But ..?"

"But for the rest of us who are doing OK with our wives and kids, this keep-your-promises thing is going to be nothing but trouble."

"How so?"

"It's simple. If women see a million men out there preaching and bragging about how they're keeping the big promises, then eventually they're going to want men - all men, including me - to keep the small ones, right?"

"That seems logical. But what's wrong with that?"

"Are you nuts? Do you know how many little promises a guy makes and breaks to his wife per day?"

"Plenty, I would guess."

"Dozens. Hundreds, maybe. If this thing gets out of hand, I might have to start picking up my underwear off the floor. I might have to start rinsing the whiskers out of the sink and putting dirty cups in the dishwasher. I might have to ... to ..."

"Go ahead," I said. "You're among friends."

"... to change the roll of toilet paper when it's empty."

My god. Not that.

My friends: the Promise Keepers must be stopped.

–October 9, 1997

Praise
the Lord
for Baptists

I called up Moon Dimple, my pal back home, to invite him
down from the Upper Peninsula for a weekend of frivolity.

"Can't," he said.

"Worms die of heat prostration again?" I said.

Moon is the proud owner of the world's only combination
funeral parlor, bait shop and gas 'n' go, and from time to time
his worms go to the great compost heap in the sky when
Moon forgets to unload them from the open bed of his pickup.

"Nope, I remembered to bring 'em in this time," he said.

"So why can't you come?"

"Got church."

"Church? They having a big bingo or something?" I said.

"Very funny," he replied. "For your information, I've become
a highly religious guy."

"And for your information," I said, "Budweiser does not in
any way, shape or form qualify as a religion, even if it is
called the king of beers."

"You took your funny pills again, I see," he said. "I'll have
you know that ever since I found religion, I haven't missed a
week at church."

"And how long has it been since you found religion?"

"More than a week now."

I was impressed. Sure, one week isn't much. But for Moon,
who once said he didn't go to church because he wasn't sure
if the word "pew" was a reference to the body odor of his

fellow congregationalists, this was stunning news. So I asked what had caused this amazing transformation.

"It ain't amazing," he said. "It's just that I've started to see the wisdom of the way."

"Well, good for you, Moon," I said heartily. "By the way, what denomination are you?"

"Baptist," he said. "Southern Baptist."

Ah, so that's it, I thought.

"This wouldn't have something to do with the Southern Baptists voting to adopt a new article saying that women should `submit graciously to the servant leadership of her husband,' now would it?"

"It doesn't have something to do with it," he said. "It has everything to do with it."

"Don't you think that's just a wee bit sexist?" I said. "After all, these are the '90s."

"All I know," he said, "is that them Southern Baptists say it says right there in the Bible that a woman ought to submit graciously unto her husband. And I figure, who am I to question the Bible?"

"So what does Sadie think?"

Sadie's his wife. She's a petite but enormously intimidating woman. Back in high school, she was voted "Best Glare."

"Oh, she's great with it," said Moon.

"In other words, she doesn't know yet, right?"

"Right. I plan on telling her soon, though."

"How soon?" I asked.

"As soon as I get a few dozen more services under my belt," he said. "I want to make sure I'm truly filled with the spirits."

"Spirits? Don't you mean spirit?"

"That, too," he said. "But that's pretty hard to come by down at Boobies."

Boobies is a tavern. No, I don't know how it got the name.

"You mean to tell me that your church meets down at Boobies?" I said. "That's shameful, Moon."

"No, it ain't," he said. "We ain't got no Southern Baptist churches up here. So me and the guys made our own church down to Boobies. We meet every Saturday night, whether we're in the mood for religion or not."

"One must have standards," I said dryly.

"One must," he repeated.

"And so what do you do at your church meetings?"

"Pray," he said.

"About what?"

"Mostly that our wives don't find out."

"Amen," I said.

"Praise the Lord," he said.

–June 17, 1998

So much for new technology

I was excited about my new home computer, so I called up Moon Dimple to tell him about it.

"It's great," I said. "It can do spreadsheets and business letters. It can do my taxes and keep track of my money. It came with this little camera that lets me do video chats with people. It can play CDs and even DVDs. It has a zippy Internet connection. It does everything a man could want a home computer to do except make me a cup of coffee. It is truly a modern marvel."

"S'great," Moon grunted. "But what do you actually do with it?"

"What do you mean what do I do with it? I just told you. It can do all of those things and more."

"Yeah," said Moon. "But I know you and I'll bet you don't do none of that stuff. For instance, do you even know what a spreadsheet is?"

I had to admit that I didn't. I'm a writer. I don't know a spreadsheet from a bed sheet.

"But it's great to know that if I ever need one, I've got one!" I said.

"Uh-huh," said Moon. "So how about business letters? You ever do any business letters at home?"

I thought for a moment and had to admit that, no, the last letter I wrote on my home computer was one to my son's teacher, which before computers I would have dashed off long-hand.

"I thought so," said Moon. "And how your taxes? You doing those on your computer?"

Well, no. I have a living, breathing fear of numbers and the IRS, so I can't see ever doing my own taxes, even with the fancy-schmancy software that came with my computer. I pay an accountant so I have someone to point a finger at in case there's something wrong. I doubt the IRS would buy it if I said, "It's the software's fault."

"I see," said Moon. "But at least you have that camera thing. You're probably getting loads of use out of that, right?"

"Uh, no," I said. "I used it once and I haven't used it since. It's pretty complicated, and the other person has to know that you're going to call, so it's not that useful."

"Hmm," Moon said. "But at least you get all that quality entertainment on it. Bet those CDs sound great."

"Not really," I said, suddenly feeling a whole lot more glum than when I'd called. "I don't play much music on it because the stereo sounds better. And I don't play DVDs very often because the screen's small and you have to sit on a chair right in front of it to see it."

"I see," said Moon. "But at least you have that zippy Internet connection. Funny, though, I wouldn't have pegged you for a big Internet guy. You're pretty impatient to be putting up with slow page loads and all the dummies in chat rooms. Good for you, though. You must be developing patience."

"Not exactly," I said, sighing. "The truth is that I was hot for the Internet at first, but that quickly became old."

Pages built too slowly, there were indeed too many morons in the chat rooms and I discovered that I could live without most of the information available on-line. In truth, I prefer reading the newspaper to surfing the Net.

"I see," said Moon. "So let's review: You have a new whiz-bang gizmo that lets you do all sorts of things that you don't want or need to do. And for this, you paid how much?"

"About $1,300," I said sheepishly.

I said something else, but I don't think he heard me over his own laughter.

–February 28, 2001

The Food Nazis strike again

You really shouldn't eat that," I said to my friend Bob Gnarly, old-fashioned American.

I was pointing at a sausage on his plate. We were eating breakfast at one of those buffet places with 16 tons of food.

"Why not?" he asked. "Did you see the cook drop it on the floor or something?"

"No. But it's sausage."

"So?"

"So sausage will kill you."

He looked at the sausage.

"Don't look so dangerous to me," he said, jabbing it with a fork and taking a bite. "Don't taste so dangerous either."

"Obviously you have missed the latest news," I said.

"News? What news? We invade Cuba or something?"

"I meant the news about the Center for Science in the Public Interest."

"Aw, jeez, not them again."

"And just what do you mean by that?" I demanded.

"They're that food Nazi group, right?"

"If you mean the Washington, D.C.-based watchdog group, then yes."

"Well, I think they're a bunch of sickos. I think they get some kinda weirdo kick out of scaring folks. Lemme guess, this time they're saying chewing gum's bad for you, right?"

"Actually, it's breakfast. They said many common breakfast foods are loaded with fat, cholesterol and salt."

"You mean like this here biscuit smothered with pork gravy?"

"My god, man, don't tell me you intend to ingest that?"

"Ingest it? Hell, no. I intend to eat it." And in three bites it was gone. I waited for him to clutch his chest and keel over dead, but nothing happened. In fact he was smiling.

"So what else did them pointy-headed killjoys say?" he said.

"They said Belgian waffles swimming in butter and syrup are about the worst possible things you can eat. If you eat just one, you are consuming three days' worth of fat."

"Great," he said, grinning. "Just think of all the time I'll save." And with that, he gulped down the waffle.

I was aghast. "How can you abuse yourself like that?" I said. "You're a heart attack waiting to happen."

"No, I'm not. Look, I ain't stupid. I don't eat like this all the time. I do it just once a week. And I enjoy it. You oughta try it."

"But my cholesterol," I whined.

"See, that's the problem right there. The doom-and-gloomers got you so worried about food you don't enjoy eating anymore. Ain't that true?"

I had to admit it was.

"And that ain't the way God intended it, son. Eating's supposed to be a joy, one of life's great pleasures. I mean, just look at what's in front of you right now."

"You mean my oatmeal and weak tea? This is what I eat every day."

"I thought so. Do you enjoy that stuff?"

"Well, no."

"So how does that make you feel?"

"A little depressed, to be honest with you."

"And ain't depression bad for you?"

"I suppose."

"And don't the doctors say if you're depressed you can eat all the oatmeal in the world and it ain't gonna do you no good?"

"Well, yes."

"Then eat, boy. Live a little. It won't kill you. Here, have a piece of my bacon."

"I don't know ..."

"Aw, go on. Don't you remember what happened to that Euell Gibbons guy?"

"Not exactly."

"He was the guy who ate pine needles and stuff on television. Said it would help him live forever."

"So."

"So the guy croaked in his bowl of twigs one morning. And I doubt he truly enjoyed a single meal his whole life. You wanna be like that?"

I said no.

For the record, the bacon was delicious.

−March 4, 1996

Bigamy?
That's big
of you

he phone rang at a quarter to midnight.

"So would you want two wives?" the voice on the other end boomed.

Ah, Moon Dimple. My childhood friend and either the dumbest smart guy on the planet or the smartest dumb guy. I'm never sure which.

You know, some people say hello before they start blabbing, I said. It's considered polite. You ever think about trying that?

"What for? You know my voice."

Deaf people in China know your voice, Moon.

"Har-de-har-har. So wouldja?"

Want to be married to two women? Why do you ask?

"Cuz I saw that article in the paper last week about the guy down in St. Clair Shores who was arrested for bigamy."

And?

"And I was just wondering what possesses a guy to do something like that."

Well, I think the answer to that is pretty clear, don't you think?

"Yeah, but still, what a price to pay."

Price?

"Yeah, you're married, you know what it's like. First, you got your honey-do list. Can you imagine having two wives coming at you with lists? You'd spend every one of your weekends painting one room or another. And when you weren't painting, you'd be wallpapering or mowing or, god forbid, going to antique shows."

True. But such is the price of love.

"Love, schmove. I wanna know how this guy handled two bouts of moodiness per month."

By that, I take it you're making a veiled reference to ... .

"Exactly, doing the bills. Man, when my wife does the bills she'll bite your head off for two days after. And what about family vacations?"

What about them?

"I just wanna know how he handled it. If Wife A wanted to go to the beach for a week, what did he tell Wife B?"

Probably he invented a business trip.

"The guy owned a hardware store. What's he supposed to be off doing, attending a hammer convention? I just don't get it. And here's another thing, how'd he deal with all the confusion?"

Confusion?

"Yeah, how did he keep everyone straight? If you've got Wife A with three kids and Wife B with two kids, how do you avoid calling Wife A Wife B or vice versa? And how would you keep your family histories straight? Say you mention that great summer vacation you had three years ago or the time you argued about leaving your socks on the floor. How would you keep it all straight who you had the good time with and who was mad at you about the socks?"

A Palm Pilot?

"Very funny. I'm serious."

I don't know, Moon. I have my hands full keeping one wife happy.

"Exactly. Every guy I know says the same thing. So what's with this guy?"

Maybe he figured he could do the impossible. Some guys are like that. Arrogant. It's a trait of our gender. Women don't have a similar arrogance. You'll notice that you never see a female bigamist.

"That's because women ain't stupid. They know being married to one person is hard enough. This guy, he must be a real piece of work. But I figure he'll get his comeuppance."

How so?

"Both them women are divorcing him."

So?

"Think about it. Two alimony payments."

—June 14, 2000

NRA idea is full of holes

You see what Moses did this week?" said Moon
Dimple.

Moon is my hometown pal. He's the smartest
dumb guy on the planet or the dumbest smart guy.
I'm never sure which.

I said: Apparently I didn't see what he did because I have
no idea what you're talking about. Did he part the Red Sea
again or something?

"Not that Moses, dummy. Charlton Heston."

Ah. And what is Mr. Heston up to these days, aside from
working to ensure that children are issued Glocks at birth?

"He got himself re-elected as the head honcho of the
National Rifle Association. But that ain't what I'm talking
about. I'm talking about the theme parks."

Theme parks?

"Yeah, he said the NRA is gonna open theme parks and
restaurants with a gun theme."

You're not serious.

"Serious as a bullet in the head. I read it in the paper.
Right there in black and white it said theme parks and
restaurants."

Wonderful. If it's one thing this country needs it's a theme
park where the kiddies can go on a ride named It's a Small
Caliber World After All.

"I know. That's exactly what I was thinking. And can you

see telling the old lady that you're packing up her and the kids to spend a week at Lock & Load World?"

No. But then my wife isn't a gun person. She doesn't believe that an armed society is a polite society. She thinks an armed society is one in which people get shot. Go figure.

"So what? You think she wouldn't wanna go on a ride like Well-Armed Pirates of the Caribbean or take a spin in the Twirling Six-Gun Holsters?"

Uh, probably not.

"Well, maybe she'd like the Swiss Cheese Family Robinson ride."

Doubtful.

"OK then, she's into history right?"

Right.

"So maybe she'd like The Hall of Presidents Who Weren't Liberal Gun Control Pansies. And at the very least, I'm sure she'd love how you and her would get around in Lock & Load World.

Tram?

"Bullet train."

Naturally. Listen, I just don't think you'll ever convince someone like her to go to a theme park glorifying guns. It's just not her thing.

"OK, then how about a restaurant? The story I read said they was gonna build one in Times Square in New York. Can't you see taking her out to a romantic dinner at Le Uzi? I guess when you get there the hostess asks if you wanna sit in the smoking or nonsmoking gun section. And instead of getting the blue plate special you can order the Saturday night special."

Sounds like a classy joint.

"And that ain't all. The story said they're gonna have `realistic' electronic shooting galleries at these restaurants."

They're going to shoot at 7-11 clerks?

"No, dummy. Stuff like deer and elk. I hear if it's successful they might let you shoot your own dinner. You know, like you pick your own lobster now. You pick a cow, step out back and blammo."

Quaint. But I doubt Marcia will want to set foot in such a place.

"Nah, me either," said Moon. "But there's one good thing."

What's that?

"At least if they got their own theme parks and restaurants, the gun nuts will all be in one place."

What's so good about that?

"Makes it easier to keep an eye on 'em."

–May 24, 2000

Moon with his head in the stars

Many social observers - mostly snooty newspaper columnists - have had great fun with the "Star Wars" buffs, who are currently all aquiver about the upcoming prequel.

They have called them geeks for camping outside movie theaters to get the first tickets for the first showing of "The Phantom Menace."

They have scoffed at them for lining up at toy stores to buy plastic dolls of characters in the movie, or for announcing their intention to see the movie dozens of times.

One newspaper columnist even scolded them, saying they'd be better off spending their time, money and energy on their children instead of acting like children themselves.

I must admit, I've taken a few shots at "Star Wars" fans myself. It does indeed seem a bit ridiculous for grown adults to get all googly-eyed over a mere movie.

In fact I said so to Moon Dimple, my buddy who is either the dumbest smart guy I know or the smartest dumb guy.

"Ridiculous?" he said. "What's ridiculous about it? So I camped out to get tickets, so what?"

Well, I said, for one thing it rained that night, didn't it?

"Well, yeah, but this one guy had a plastic tarp, and this woman she had some hot chocolate in a big Thermos, and someone else had a deck of cards. So we sat around under the tarp and talked and laughed and played euchre. It was actually kind of fun. What'd you do last night?"

Um, well, I fell asleep watching a ballgame on TV.

"Mmm, sounds like big fun," he said. "As Yoda would say, `Boring you are. Dull your life is.'"

My life's not dull, I protested. And at least I don't go around spouting the wit and wisdom of characters who are nothing more than flickering images on a screen.

"Oh, no? Aren't you the one who said to me the other day, `Moon, 90 percent of baseball is half mental'?"

Yes. So?

"So that's Yogi Berra."

Right. So?

"So do you know Yogi Berra?"

You mean personally? No.

"So really, he's no more real to you than Yoda is to me."

I suppose not.

"And I'll assume you've never met him, right? You've only ever seen him on TV?"

Right.

"So to you he's really just a flickering image on a screen. So what's the difference between you quoting Yogi and me quoting Yoda?"

All right, all right, I said. But what about all those "Star Wars" toys you went and bought the other day. You said you spent $150. That's ridiculous. Don't you have anything better to do with your money?"

"Actually, no. Listen, I pay my bills. I pay a mortgage. My kids got food to eat. So I use a little leftover to have some fun, so what? What do you do with your extra money?"

If there is any, I normally send it off to my broker to be invested in mutual funds.

"That's it?"

No. I buy bonds, too.

"I mean, don't you have any fun with your money? You know, just waste some for the heck of it?"

Sure, I said. In fact I just bought some lawn fertilizer.

"Whoo, boy. Stand back. Here comes Mr. Fun."

Well, I may not be Mr. Fun, I said. But at least I act my age.

"That's fine. You go ahead and act your age. Me, I'll have some fun. Gotta go now. My buddies and I are off to buy some more toys, then I'm dressing up like Darth Vader for a costume party. By the way, what are you doing tonight?"

Spreading fertilizer, I said.

"You're a wild man," he said.

And then he hung up laughing.

–May 16, 1999

Gonna die?
Better be
famous

The phone rang, I answered, and without so much as a hello, the voice said, "So if you was Mr. Bessette would you be ticked off right about now?"

Ah, Moon Dimple, my childhood pal who is either the smartest dumb guy I know or the dumbest smart guy. I'm never sure which.

Hello to you, too, I said.

"Oh yeah, hi. So would you be ticked?"

Ticked? I don't even know who you're babbling about.

"Of course you don't. Hardly anyone does. That's because they wasn't famous on their own like ol' John-John there. Them Bessette kids was just along for the ride, so to speak."

Ah, I've got it now. You mean Carolyn Bessette Kennedy, JFK Jr.'s wife, and her sister Lauren, right? I believe since both of them died, yes, if I were Mr. Bessette I'd be a little upset.

"No, no," said Moon. "I mean, would you be ticked off at the talking heads on TV?"

For what?

"For treating those poor women like they was them bum steerage passengers on the Titanic."

I guess I hadn't noticed that they had.

"You ain't been watching then. Every time Dan Rather or Peter Jennings or Larry King talked about the plane crash, it was JFK this and JFK that. About the only time they mentioned the Bessettes was when they started feeling guilty about their own overkill. Then they'd say something like, `Of course we can't forget that there were two other people on that flight.' But that's baloney because they're the ones who DID forget 'em. Am I right?"

Perhaps. But JFK was the son of a president. There's just naturally more interest in him.

"Yeah, sure. But I'll bet you if one of Gerald Ford's kids came up missing the networks wouldn't interrupt programming for hours and hours like they did. They'd break in, tell us about what happened, then get back to showing the golf match. And you know why?"

No, why?

"Because they aren't as pretty as John-John."

Oh, come on.

"No, really. Remember how People magazine called him the sexiest man alive?"

Yes, but ...

"Well, you think there'd be this much hoo-ha if he wasn't handsome? No way. Ask any of Lyndon Johnson's kids."

You're quite insane, I said.

"No, but this country is nuts. Look at the fuss everyone is making over this. And for what? The guy wasn't a senator. He wasn't a brilliant scientist. He was a guy who ran a struggling magazine and was a celebrity through no fault of his own. That's it. That's all."

Unbelievable, I said. You're running down a dead guy?

"No I'm not," Moon said. "I'm sad he's gone. He seemed like the nicest Kennedy there ever was, including his dad. So nice, in fact, that he'd probably be mad that the media is treating his wife and her sister like after-thoughts."

Interesting point, I said.

"You know what I'd do if I were their dad? I'd call up Dan Rather and say, `Hey, wait a minute, my daughters may not have had a famous dad, but they were pretty special, too.'"

Yes, I bet you would.

"And then I'd say, `Hey, Dan, how about you use some of MY old photos of my girls when they was kids, and talk to THEIR old pals and teachers about how great they were, and then do a teary retrospective of THEIR lives, like you did for John-John?'"

And what do you think his response would be?

"Ha, he'd tell me, `No chance, pal. This is great TV.' That's the lesson here, I guess."

Lesson? What lesson?

"That if you're gonna die in this country, make sure you're not with someone who's good-looking and famous when you do it.

¬*June 25, 1999*

Camping
is second
nature to Biff

My friend Biff Johansen decided to go camping up north, so he sat down to make a list of the things he might need to ensure his survival in the great outdoors.

The list included the usual: tent, sleeping bags, canteen, waterproof matches, a large knife.

"Very impressive," I said. "You sound like you're really going to rough it."

"Nah," he said. "That junk's for the kids. They like to pitch the tent under the awning of the RV."

With that, he loaded his wife, kids and gear into the family's 40-foot Windstream, and together they hit the open road, looking for a break from the great American rat race.

As luck would have it, though, 10 miles later he was in a long, snaking back-up on northbound I-75 with everybody else who was hitting the open road in their RV looking for a break from the great American rat race.

That kind of thing would irritate me to the point of exploding. But Johansen is made from calmer stuff. Instead of huffing and puffing and leaning on his horn as I would have done, he simply shifted the RV into park, leapt from his captain's chair, popped a copy of "Toy Story II" into the VCR and waited out the traffic jam in style.

"We've seen it a million times," he said cheerfully, munching microwave popcorn. "But when you're on the road, you got to rough it."

Hours later, the Johansen family pulled into the welcome center of Woods R Us, the rustic, backwoods campground they've visited every summer since they discovered it just off the interstate back in 1991.

"Remember the first year, honey?" Biff said. "They hadn't even blacktopped the campsites yet." Mrs. Johansen smiled and looked wistful.

This year, the Johansens were in luck. The clerk said their favorite site, old No. 435, was available. They like it because it's only a short walk to the campground's all-night bistro/latte bar but far enough away from the lake so that the sound of all the croaking frogs and jumping fish doesn't disturb their sleep.

After hooking the Windstream to the camp's electric, water and sewage systems, Biff decided the family needed to unwind from the long, stressful trip, during which the RV's CD and Nintendo systems had gone on the blink.

"I'll tell you what, kids. You jump on your bikes and head on over to the pool while your mother and I get the Explorer off the tow-bar and head into town and pick up a pizza."

"Yaaay!" squealed the kids. And off they sped.

"It's good to see them so excited about camping," said Biff, throwing a satisfied arm around his wife's shoulder.

He was feeling so happy and content that after picking up the pizza, as an extra surprise for the kids, he bought some S'mores ice cream and a tape of campfire songs for the family to listen to that evening as they played euchre around the dining room table.

That evening a fine time was had by all. After the cards had been played and the ice cream gobbled, the kids and Mrs. Johansen drifted off to bed.

Not Biff, though. He flipped on the air conditioning, leaned back in his Naugahyde chair and popped the top of an imported beer from the refrigerator. Then he loosened his belt, tuned the satellite dish to a late-night West Coast ballgame and let out a big, satisfied sigh.

"Ah, it's good to get back to nature," he said to himself, just before drifting off to a peaceful frogless sleep.

¬*July 20, 2001*

^{Of}Jocks
^{and}Jerks

Tiger Stadium's last turn at bat

I am tired now.

My bones ache with rust. My skin is flaking and falling off. I sag here, sag there. When people look at me now, try as they might, they don't see the vital young thing I used to be, way back when. They see an old lady. An old lady they love. An old lady on whom much paint has been slathered over the years, like too much rouge on your grandmother. An old lady of whom they have many wonderful memories. But an old lady, still. And we all know what happens to old ladies.

I am Tiger Stadium.

I am 87.

And soon I will die.

At least as a ballpark, I will. The Tigers, my Tigers, will take up with another ballpark come the spring, tossing me aside like a used hot dog wrapper.

That's how it goes, I suppose. The old give way to the young. I do hope I am given the respect due the elderly, though.

They tell me that I may yet serve another purpose. They may gut me and stuff me with loft apartments. (Can you imagine?)

They may preserve me as sort of a living museum, a field of dreams, where youngsters can chase the ghosts of Mickey Cochrane, Charlie Gehringer, Ty Cobb and Hank Greenberg, who still run and slide and pitch and swing within me.

They may even knock me down and let me rest in peace.

Any of those things would be fine. I'm not particular.

The only thing I fear is nothing. That they will not find the money to fix me up for another purpose, but yet will lack the will to demolish me.

I shudder at the thought of sitting here rotting as people pass by saying, "Isn't it a shame? She used to be so nice."

And I did used to be nice, you know. When I opened on April 12, 1912, (they called me Navin Field back then) the 23,000 people who came to me, who watched my Tigers whip the Cleveland Indians 6-5, thought I was a real swank dame.

Especially compared to Bennett Park. That's what my forerunner on this very same site was called. It came to be in 1896 when George Arthur Vanderbeck, who owned my Tigers at the time, bought the land here at Michigan and Trumbull, leveled the dirt, threw down some grass seed, put up some wood bleachers and birthed a baseball tradition.

Cobb played there, you know? Tyrus Raymond Cobb. The Georgia Peach. The orneriest man to ever play the game.

He played there, when fans used to stand four deep around the waist-high outfield fences and watch and smoke and cheer and jeer.

He played in me, too. At the time, I only seated 5,000 people. But by 1925, when Cobb celebrated his 20th year as a Tiger, they had long since added another 25,000 seats. And a press box.

I've been a work in progress ever since.

In 1937, they gave me a two-story grandstand in right field. Then the next year they added them in center and left. And over the next 50 years, they ringed me with lights, surrounded me with aluminum, changed my name again. They even added on something called a Tigers Den.

I mention this so you will know how I came to look the way I do today. I am like an old crazy quilt stitched together by your aunt. A piece of this. A piece of that. A bit here. A bit there.

OK, I'll admit I'm not much of a looker. What was it Al Kaline once said I looked like? A battleship? What did Alan Trammell and Lance Parrish think I was when they first saw me? A warehouse?

I know that some people see me from the freeway, see my shape, my light stands, my flagpoles flying banners from the other teams, the Orioles, the Blue Jays, the Yankees. They see this conglomeration, and to them I resemble a giant, gray, ugly, shabby birthday cake.

I know they've been coming into me these past few years, seen my old-fashionedness, sneered at my deficiencies and said, "When are they going to dump this dog? When are they going to build a new stadium with all sorts of do-dads and tin-twanglers?"

But I notice that many of these same people have been coming back lately, strolling through me, breathing my smells, drinking in my sights.

One last time, they all say.

And that's fine. I don't mind indulging them, just as I don't mind dying. It happens to us all. I have had a good, long life.

Babe Ruth hit his longest home run here. Lou Gehrig ended his streak here. Al Kaline roamed my right field corner. Kirk Gibson thrilled my fans. Mark Fidrych? Oh, my.

I have hosted World Series, title fights, concerts, political rallies. I even hosted the Detroit Lions for 29 years. Many people forget that.

Those are the things, incidentally, that most people have focused on in these my final days - the wondrous things that have happened on my field of play. But you know what I'm most proud of?

The moment.

The moment when a young fan first emerges from the tunnels and catwalks beneath my stands and glimpses my playing field, my emerald carpet, and for a millisecond is transfixed, awestruck.

I have provided millions of such moments over the years. Millions.

I am Tiger Stadium.

I am 87.

I will die soon.

Remember me.

–September 26, 1999

It ain't booyah to me

t is late and I am flipping back and forth between two sports networks.

This is what I hear:

"And Johnson put the biscuit in the basket faster than the guy at the airport puts shiiiiiine on a shoe!"

"Then, second quarter, Williams took it home like he was late for dinner and - booyah! - he's thinking, 'I'm so good, I'm smoother than BUTTAH!'"

"Oh my, he is cooler than the other side of the pillow."

"Annhegoes duuuuuu-eep! Ovahduh leff-feel waaaaaaahl!"

Here is what I am thinking:

Biscuit? Pillow? Booyah?

Huh?

Maybe it was me. It was late. I was tired. But what they said didn't match at all what I was watching. I was watching, in order:

A clip of a toothless hockey player scoring.

A clip of a college basketball player scoring.

A clip of a professional basketball player, who had just scored, twitching like someone had connected electrodes to his toenails and turned the juice on high.

Mark McGwire hitting a home run.

What's happened to sports broadcasting? Not so many years ago, the sports broadcaster was the guy on the news team who wore the worst jacket. He was always named Chip or Al. He tended to be glib, but other than that his delivery was the same as everyone else's.

He would ruffle some papers and say in a loud voice (sportscasters are always loud), "The Tigers defeated the Indians 6-4 tonight. Josh McLooney hit a home run. And in hockey ..."

It was dry but at least you knew who won the game and why.

Today they're all Chuckles the Clown. They do everything short of pulling out a seltzer bottle and squirting the camera. They shout, they criticize, they all work way too hard to be wry or snide or funny. And every single one of them dreams of coming up with a signature catch phrase that they will be remembered for.

These catch phrases used to be of the Ernie Harwell "It's loooong gone" variety, which was fine because it pertained to the game. But "booyah!"? What the heck does that have to do anything?

As always, I think things would be better if I were in charge. If I owned a sports network, I would set my station apart by gathering all the sportscasters in a room and saying something like:

"You, the shouter. Stop shouting. Or else. And you, the guy with the unnaturally dark tan, no more tanning booths for you. And from now on I want to understand every single word you say or you're outta here.

"And you, lady. What's with the wisecracks and the smirks? Knock it off. You wanna make jokes, go find a comedy club.

"And you, Keith Olbermann, from Fox Sports. I know you became famous for inserting criticisms and smarmy, smug commentary during the highlights, but it's getting a little old, OK? If you hate athletes that much, if you think you're so above it all, go the heck back to MSNBC and its 47 viewers.

"And all of you, from now on I want scores and clear, understandable descriptions of the clips you are showing. You are to call a home run a home run. And the first one to describe anything as 'buttah!' gets traded to the Home Shopping Network for a Cuisinart. Now everyone repeat after me: 'People watch sports shows for the highlights, not for the announcers.' "

After all, that other stuff - the lame attempts at humor, the flaccid criticisms - is why we have newspaper columnists.

–April 24, 2000

I confess:
I hate the
Olympics

Today, I come out of the closet: I am an Olympics Grinch.

I sit up here on my Grinchy mountain and I hear all the TV sets down in Whoville blaring the Olympic theme and I hear the happy oohing and aahing of the people, and I think, "There must be a way to keep the Olympics from continuing this year. There must!"

I hate the Olympics. I hate everything about them. I hate the sports. I hate the breathless announcers, who get so excited you'd swear they'd never seen anyone swim before. I especially hate the sappy little biographies of the athletes, every single one of whom has overcome some "Great Tragedy" and "Sacrificed Everything" to "Triumph on the World Stage of Olympic Sport."

Gag me. I am not running down these people. I guess there's something admirable about their dedication and all. But when I see people who dedicate their lives to ping-pong or pole vaulting or, god forbid, water polo, I can't help but think, "Get a job, wouldja?"

Maybe my heart is two sizes too small. Maybe I have an attitude because it's freezing up here on my mountain and my animators gave me no pants. Or maybe I've simply watched too many Olympiads.

Whatever the reason, I think the Olympics are one big bore, the kind of second-rate, marginally interesting sports most of us play in high school then leave behind.

Remember cross-country? I was a cross-country runner in high school. What possessed me to do such a thing, I'll never know. At my high school, cross-country was for all the guys who weren't big enough or fast enough for the football team. It was a lonely, odd sport. The only people who showed up for a cross-country meet were our coach and our parents.

We had cheerleaders once, at one meet. The football coach made them come. As I passed by them I heard one say to another, "Why do they DO this?" That's how I feel when I watch the Olympic triathlon. Why do they do that? What's the point? And why do we as a nation suddenly pretend to care? We don't really, you know. Otherwise we'd have "Monday Night Triathlon."

And many Olympic sports aren't even sports. They're activities.

Can't tell the difference? Here, let me help:

Archery? Activity.

Table tennis? Activity.

Equestrian? Activity. (And if it's a sport, then I say the medals should go to the horses. They're the ones doing all the work.)

Canoeing? Please.

Beach volleyball? Dude, come on. Can you tell me that an American victory in beach volleyball would fill you with patriotic fervor?

Air rifle? I'm not even sure that qualifies as an activity.

This is where you write me nasty letters saying, "You cretin, it takes a lot of talent to be good at air rifle. Bet you couldn't do it."

You're right. I couldn't. Nor would I want to. I had a BB gun when I was a kid, but I got over it. Just because some people become good at something doesn't make it a sport. And if it does, then how come Nintendo 64 isn't an Olympic sport? Lots of kids are good at that.

And while I'm ranting, let me say this: Bob Costas must die.

Thank you.

Now give me that roast beast. I'm taking it with me.

–September 20, 2000

Recognizing your own greatness

You can't see me, but I am a dancing machine here. Hip-wiggle, shake, groove, KICK!

Why am I dancing? I am dancing because I just finished getting myself a cup of coffee.

Didn't spill a drop.

Yeeeeeeeeees! High-five, baby! We bad! We bad!

This is my new thing. Every time I complete a task in my work day, no matter how mundane, I celebrate.

For instance, you should have seen me after I successfully wiped away the dust that collects on my computer screen. I charged at one of my co-workers for a jublilant flying chest bump. As it turns out, it probably wasn't the best idea, judging from the look on her face as she picked herself up off the floor. But you get the picture.

This idea for shameless public self-celebration hit me during the Super Bowl. There I was watching the game when I noticed that after every other play, no matter how routine or unspectacular, the players would leap up and begin twitching and hollering like someone had dropped a live weasel down their pants.

One player, for instance, returned a kick 30 yards. Which is good but not great. And yet he jumped up and began screaming and jabbing his finger at the other team.

Another player, after making a sack, pretended his fingers were six-shooters. "Kchew! Kchew!" he went.

A wide receiver, after he scored, stuffed the ball over the goalpost. And when he landed he wiggled like Jell-O.

Another didn't even wait until he scored to celebrate. As he approached the goal line with the ball, he slowed and duck-walked in. Which was bad enough, but then it occurred to me that he must have practiced it, because you don't just DO something like that.

Now, normally, as a lifelong sports fan, this sort of behavior would disgust me. I like my sports straight. I don't like spikes or dances or any of that "I'm No. 1" garbage. When they reach the endzone, football players, as one analyst once said, should act like they've been there before.

And they certainly shouldn't be celebrating ordinary plays. Doing what you do then dusting yourself off and walking away to go do it again, that's called professionalism.

Then I got to thinking, hey, why not try it before I criticize it. Walk a mile in their jockstraps, so to speak.

So that's what I've been doing. And I must say, I like it.

The other day, for instance, I successfully adjusted the height of my chair by moving this little lever on the bottom.

Normally, after performing this incredible feat, I would, you know, sit down. This time, however, I did a series of backflips into the center of the office, where I performed a couple of butt waggles followed by a he-man arm-clenching thing. I thought I was very impressive. But I must say, the reaction of my co-workers wasn't what I expected.

Instead of cheering wildly, they fell silent and stared. One of them muttered, "It finally happened. He's flipped."

I reminded them that I was only emulating the behavior of the athletes they adore. But they continued to stare. Several backed away nervously. One reached for a phone.

No matter. I felt empowered. I felt actualized. I felt like the best darned chair adjuster ever. I felt as if, sooner or the later, the world would come to recognize my chair-adjusting greatness and would then understand and support my self-enthusiasm.

And that's exactly what I told the security people when they came to get me.

–February 2, 1997

Tides rise, golfers hack

I f you are a golfer, there is a legal case about which you should be highly alarmed. Especially if you are a golfer like I am.

What kind of golfer am I?

Well, let's just say my golfing partners refer to me as Sgt. Heller because I am always marching to the right, to the left, to the right after my wayward golf ball.

That is to say that I rarely if ever play from the portion of the golf course commonly referred to as "the fairway."

On good days, I play "the rough," which is that area of the course to the left and right of the fairway with long grass and trees obstructing one's view of the green.

On bad days, I play the "far rough" also known, in technical golfing terminology, as "out of bounds." Out of bounds consists of forests, streams and cornfields as well as the back yards, decks and flower beds of nearby homes and condominiums.

Anyway, I have many, many more bad days than good, which is why I am so concerned about Eileen Hennessey.

She is the Rhode Island condo owner who is suing a golfer for hitting her with a golf ball. It happened seven years ago. Michael Pyne lost control of a shot and it smacked Hennessey in the head as she gardened, giving her a concussion.

Like any self-respecting American, Hennessey sued. The Rhode Island Superior Court initially threw out the suit but the state Supreme Court recently reinstated it, saying Pyne "has a duty to exercise reasonable care for the safety of those people who may be located within" range of a shot.

So now Hennessey's case will go to trial.

Golfers, do you realize what this means? If Hennessey wins, we may someday be held legally and financially responsible for the behavior of our golf balls. (Next thing you know we'll be responsible for our teenagers. Errant golf balls, errant teenagers, what's the difference?)

This could be bad, the end of golf as we know it, since most of us have no idea where our shots (or our teens) are going.

I certainly don't. I HOPE I know where it is going. I PLAN for it to go a certain somewhere. I have the very best of INTENTIONS for it. But in truth, I don't know where it's going or what it will do when it gets there. What do I look like, Jack Nicklaus?

I say if a golf ball of mine goes astray and conks a condo owner in the head, it's just as much his fault as mine.

Who bought the condo, huh? If you bought a home next to a mortar range, would you sue when things got noisy?

Of course not. You'd know that mortars go boom. That is the natural and normal behavior for mortars.

Well, the same goes for golfers. You can no more expect golfers not to stray shots than you can expect the tide not to rise. Tides rise, golfers hack. That's all there is to it.

If Hennessey's madness is successful, you watch, golf will change. Any golfer not able to demonstrate the ability to hit nine out of 10 balls onto the fairway will be required to buy insurance. (I might not be allowed to play at all, unless Lloyd's of London steps in.)

Courses may have to string tall nets the length of the fairway. Condo associations will issue helmets.

As that famous golfer Rodney King once observed, "Can't we all just get along?"

I say we can. I say what we need is a major redesign of every golf course in the country bordered by homes or condos. What we do is uproot these homes and put them smack in the middle of the fairway. That way the Eileen Hennesseys of the world can be outside in total safety.

We're talking fairway, after all.

Your average golfer, no way he'll hit them there.

¬June 16, 1997

Today's kids
are strangers
to baseball

t is spring. I am here!" said baseball to the boy. "Rejoice!
Rejoice!"

"Who the heck are you?" said the boy to baseball. "Go
away. My momma don't want me talking to strangers."

Baseball was aghast.

"Stranger? Son, I'm no stranger. I am the game of baseball.
I am the harbinger of spring, the wellspring of joy in a young
boy's heart, the stuff of dreams. Don't you recognize me?"

The boy looked baseball up and down.

"Yeah, you look kinda familiar I guess. I seen you on TV a
coupla times. You're the one with the stick and the ball and
the guys in the funny pants, right?"

"Funny pants?" said baseball. "Those aren't funny pants.
They're knickers. And it's not a stick, it's called a bat. Haven't
you ever played me?"

The boy scoffed.

"Yeah, once. But it was boring."

Baseball winced.

"Boring? But I am this country's pastime, the American
dream played out on a grand green stage. I am glory and
passion and memories. I am Henry Aaron stroking number
762. I am Jackie Robinson stealing home. I am Kirk Gibson
limping around the bases in the World Series. I am Roy
Hobbs. I am "Field of Dreams." For crying out loud, son, I am
Babe Ruth. Surely you know the great Babe Ruth."

"Course I do," said the boy. "That's the candy bar."

"Candy bar? Son, I'm talking about the one and only Sultan of Swat, the Great Bambino!"

"The Sultan of Swat? Sure, yeah, I know him. I saw him last week on the WWF Monster Slam. He was tag-team partners with The Head Grinder and The Meat Cleaver Zombie Lunatic. Dude, he's awesome!"

Baseball looked perplexed.

"This is unbelievable. Babe Ruth is one of the greatest baseball players of all time."

"Oh, yeah," said the boy. "So how come I never heard of him? Does he gotta commercial?"

"A commercial?"

"Yeah, you know, for like sneakers or pop or something."

"Well, no," said baseball. "But ...

"Then he can't be all that great," said the boy. "Listen, I gotta go. I got soccer practice."

"Soccer practice?" said baseball, shocked. "But soccer is a European game. American boys don't play soccer."

The boy looked at baseball funny.

"You some kinda nut or something? Everyone plays soccer."

"They do?" said baseball.

"Sure," said the boy. "That and hoops."

"Hoops?"

"You know, basketball. Man, where you been?"

"But surely after you are done playing soccer you rush home and play baseball with a ball made of tape and a broken bat you found in the trash and screwed back together. That's an American rite of passage."

The boy said: "You ain't got no kids, do you? After soccer, we play Sega."

"Sega?" said baseball. "Is that another European sport?"

"No, man," said the boy. "It's a video game. You know, where you shoot stuff."

Baseball shook its head.

"OK, but THEN you play baseball, right?"

"No," said the kid. "Then we play roller hockey."

"And then baseball?"

"No, then we play Pokemon or fool around on the Internet or listen to MP3s. Later, dude. I gotta fly."

And off the boy walked.

Baseball watched him go. Then softly he began to sing.

"Take me out to the ballgame, " he whispered to an audience of no one. "Take me out to the crowd ..."

–April 9, 2000

There's no crying in sports

I cried when each of my three children were born.

They were tears of joy.

I cried when my dad died. They were tears of sorrow.

I cried when I slid into a picker bush when I was a little kid and cut up my knee. And I really let 'er rip when my dad got home that evening.

Those were tears of "Maybe if I wail hard enough he'll buy me the new Fantastic Four comic book."

But that's it. Other than those few instances, I have largely lived a tear-free life.

Great. Yet another reason I'll never make it as a pro athlete.

Have you seen all the sports blubbering going on these days? You can't tune in the highlights without a shot of some professional sweater somewhere breaking into tears at a press conference because he/she:

Won the game.

Lost the game.

Made it to the Hall of Fame.

Didn't make it to the Hall of Fame.

Retired.

Unretired.

Had his/her net worth fall below $10 million.

I won't pretend to know why the modern athlete feels the need to cry publicly, but I do have a theory. (Hey. It's what I do.) I think, given the intensity and breadth of sports coverage these days, athletes have come to believe that they are incredibly important people.

Moreover, they seem utterly convinced that we are all vitally interested in not only what they do on the field but their emotional states as well.

But I could be wrong. Most professional jocks are in their 20s and 30s, so it could be a generational thing.

Most of them were raised during the flowering of feminism in this country, so maybe that's it.

Before that, it was widely considered unmanly to cry publicly. You never saw John Wayne cry, for instance. You never saw Dick Butkus cry.

But feminists encouraged men to get "in touch" with their feelings, and now that they've started touching them they can't stop.

The most recent example was also the most horrifying.

I've been a lifelong Green Bay Packers fan, owing to my Upper Peninsula upbringing. My current favorite Packer is Brett Favre, the quarterback. He's a rough, tough guy who doesn't sit out of a game for anything short of an amputated leg. In that sense, he's a throwback.

Several weeks ago, he hurt his thumb. Then during last weekend's game he hurt it again, so badly, in fact, that he couldn't feel the ball. He kept playing anyway, and he won the game with a last-second throw.

Hot dang, I thought. Now THERE'S a sports hero for you.

Then came the post-game press conference.

Oh, yes, he cried. A reporter asked him a question and he started weeping like a willow.

At first, I didn't have a clue why. I thought maybe someone asked him about his boyhood dog, Shep, who was killed while pushing young Brett out of the path of a speeding car.

But as it turns out, he was - get this - crying because he was so amazed at his own courage for playing through the pain. Aw, jeez. That's enough to make me give up sports watching for good.

I don't know. I've never considered myself a macho guy, a man who thinks men aren't supposed to show their feelings.

But maybe that's what I am. Maybe I'm the one with the problem. Maybe I need to get in step with the modern athlete instead of carping about what a big crybaby he is.

Maybe I need to ... oh, look, I'm nearing the end of this column. The very end. This will be the last time I'll ever. ...

Sniff.

Hang on, I need a moment here, OK?

–September 15, 1999

Too bad there's no gold medal for manners

I have decided that what is good enough for the U.S. Olympic team is good enough for me.

Therefore ... hrrrrrrrk-ptoooooey!

That's me, spitting at you.

You love me now, right?

No? OK, then maybe you'll like this better:

[Editor's note: You can't see Heller right now, but he has ripped off his shirt and is flexing his muscles and making funny faces as if to communicate the fact that he is either a macho kind of guy or that he is constipated. With him it's hard to tell. He also seems to have an American flag wrapped around his head like a turban ... oh, wait, and now he's ... oh god, he's blowing his nose with it.]

There. Aren't I great? Man, I could just kiss myself ... mmmwuh, mmmwuh, mmmwuh! Much love to me. I'm the man! Whoohoo!

Hey, come back here. Don't be disgusted. I'm just imitating my new role models, our wonderful U.S. Olympians.

You didn't see?

Then let me recap just a few incidents for you:

Before each heat of the 50-meter freestyle competition, American swimmer Amy Van Dyken, the defending champion, spat into the lanes of her competitors to "intimidate" them. To me, that's gross, not intimidating, but either way it didn't work. Van Dyken not only didn't get a medal, she said of the woman who did win: "I could swim that fast if I was a man (too)."

After winning the 4x100-meter track relay, the men's team spent several minutes mugging and posing and flexing for cameras as the crowd hissed and whistled in disgust. They also used American flags to do everything but wipe their underarms. Later, one relay member mugged for cameras over the shoulder of sprinter Michael Lewis, who, ironically, was doing an interview at the time about how important it was for him to be a good representative of his country.

Members of the victorious U.S. men's basketball team goofed around and snapped photos while on the medal stand.

Swimmer Gary Hall Jr. and hurdler James Carter taunted their opponents before their respective competitions.

Now, in the past, I might have thought that such behavior was at best boorish, at worst appalling. Especially at the Olympics, where goodwill and good sportsmanship are supposedly more important than winning.

I might even have felt ashamed for my country. After all, such actions reflect on us as a nation and a people. So what does that mean the rest of the world thinks of us now - that we're a bunch of no-class jerks? Probably.

I might even have suggested that these athletes be banned for life from representing America in any sporting competition anywhere and that the only thing they should represent from this point forward is their own gargantuan, selfish egos.

But then I thought, "Aw, what the heck. It's a new hip-hop, me-good, blank-you millennium." Holding onto notions about respecting your opponent and maintaining dignity, especially when you're competing on behalf of an entire nation, that's old-fashioned.

One must swim with the tide. So I salute my American Olympians and thank them for my new lean-mean World Wrestling Federation-like attitude.

I'm your columnist.

Hrrrrrk-ptoooey!

Love me.

–October 4, 2000

So You Wanna Be _a Yooper

So You Wanna Be_aYooper

Kicking tail in the Upper Peninsula

The tourism season is nearly upon us here in Michigan, so I thought I would reprint a list of rules for downstaters (aka mittenheads, fudgies and trolls) who are planning to visit my homeland, the Upper Peninsula.

Some of the rules, received via e-mail, were written by an unknown Yooper (probably Toivo, or perhaps Oino) who has long experience with the rampaging tourist hordes that take over the U.P. come summer. A few were tweaked by me. Either way, you would be wise to heed them.

To visiting trolls:

1. Don't try to order filet mignon or pasta primavera at the Union 76 truck stop in St. Ignace. It's a diner. They serve breakfast 24 hours a day to truckers. Order something stupid, and the ladies in the kitchen will kick your butt.

2. While here, don't laugh at the names of our little towns - such as Negaunee, Ishpeming, L'Anse, Watersmeet, Kiva and Traunick. We get tired of it and of telling stupid lowlanders such as yourself what the names mean. Violate this rule and we will kick your butt.

3. Don't order a bottle or can of "soda" while here. Up here it's called "pop." Accept it. Not doing so can lead to another butt-kicking.

4. Don't refer to us as a bunch of hicks. Most of us are better educated than you is, and a heckuva lot nicer, too. But

not so nice that we won't kick your butt if you violate this rule. You hear?

5. Be nice to our business people and don't assume they're backwater rubes just because they choose to live and work here where they aren't likely to get rich. We have plenty of business sense. Just look at all the Yooper crap we sold you. If you don't agree, can you say, "Hello, Mr. Butt-Kicking"?

6. We are fully aware of how much snow we get, so shut up about it. Just spend your money and get out or we'll kick your butt. Oh, by the way, thank you for your business.

7. Don't order the vegetarian special at the local diner. Everyone will instantly know you're a tourist. Eat your steak well-done like God intended and have some potatoes with that. Also, don't ask what a pasty is or we'll REALLY kick your butt.

8. For the love of Mike, please don't try to fake a Yooper accent while visiting us. We don't have accents. You have accents. You don't agree? Well, then which side of your butt do you want kicked first - the left or the right?

9. Don't ridicule our mannerisms or way of living. We only speak when spoken to (like Mama said to). We hold open doors for others (like Mama said to). And we offer our seats to old people (like Mama said to). We do these things because A) We're nice, and B) Because if we didn't, Mama would rise from the grave and kick our sorry butts. Please assume we will do likewise to you if you fail to act accordingly.

10. Don't tell us that we left our truck running at the grocery store. We know. We do it all the time. Up here, we know no one will steal it. We don't lock our doors at night either because we don't have to. Anyone who breaks in knows they'd be in for a royal butt-kicking.

So there you have it. Enjoy your stay up north. And don't worry. Yoopers actually aren't very violent, except to deer. We just talk big, is all. We're actually fun-loving, peace-loving folks.

And if you don't agree, well, you know what'll happen.

–April 23, 2001

Rules for getting along with Yoopers

Your education, apparently, is not yet complete.
A week ago, I presented a list of rules for downstaters to follow when visiting my homeland, the Upper Peninsula, this coming summer and fall. The list was so popular I've been asked when I'm going to write more.

Well ... how about now?

Troll Rules, Part II:

1. The food with which the U.P. is most closely associated is the pasty. It's pronounced pass-tee, not paste-tee. A paste-tee is the little covering strippers wear over their whatzits. (And, no, we don't have any of those up here either - strippers, we mean.) Get it straight or we'll kick your butt.

2. Don't assume that a Yooper knows every other person who now lives or has ever lived up here. There are several hundred thousand of us, OK? We don't all know your second cousins who lived for two years "up near Watersmeet." Knock it off or we'll kick your butt royally.

3. Don't come up here camping then gripe about the black flies or mosquitos. Think of them like we do: Black flies, mosquitos and trolls who ask stupid questions are just facts of life. Might as well get used to it. (And, of course, if you don't, then we'll kick your butt.)

4. Look, we don't care about the stupid Detroit Lions, OK? Ninety percent of us are Green Bay Packers fans. Don't talk to

us about the Lions, don't complain about the lack of news about them in our newspapers, and above all, don't try to change the channel when watching football in one of our fine drinking establishments or we will most assuredly kick your butt six ways to Sunday. (Unless of course da Pack is playin' the Lions.)

5. Please don't try to talk like us because even we don't talk like us. In truth, every Yooper does not say "eh?" or "You betcha" all the time. Some of us do, some of us don't. It's true that we say "da" instead of "the," "yah" instead of yes, and we drop our G's, as in "Holy wuh, I was freezin' my tookus off when I was out fishin'. But don't you try to talk that way. We can always tell a true Yooper from a pretend Yooper and we don't like it. Butt-kicking guaranteed.

6. Stop griping about how we don't have freeways up here, except for that troll one that goes up to da Soo. If you'd learn how to drive a little faster and stop looking around for deer, the roads would be perfectly adequate. And, please, leave your road-hogging RVs and trailers at home, eh? We gotta get to work. Failure to heed this rule will result in a major league butt-kicking.

7. Listen up, we're only going to tell you once: They're pronounced like this: Mack-uh-naw (the bridge), Mack-uh-nack (the fort), Tuh-kwa-men-non (the falls), On-toe-nah-gun (the town). Get 'em right or a butt-kicking soon will follow.

8. Stop asking when we're going to try for statehood again. That Superior stuff was just propaganda we dreamed up to get you to send us more of your lovely tax dollars. We will kick your butt AND your dog's butt if you don't stop.

9. Yeah, so your cellphone doesn't work up here. Where do you think you are, Detroit? Just one little whine and thy butteth shall be kicketh.

10. And please don't ask "So where are all the bears?" or we'll strip you naked, cover you in lard and turn you loose in the woods to find out for yourself.

After we kick your butt, of course.

–May 21, 2001

Shoveling tips from da Great White North

I don't often feel pity. I don't often describe people as pitiful.

But last week during the big snowstorm, I could feel no other feeling, could describe the horror I witnessed using no other word.

The scene: the end of a driveway in my South Burton neighborhood.

The object of my pity: a neighbor who shall remain nameless for fear he would be driven from polite society.

He was out there hacking at that big, gnarly, icy furrow of snow that the snowplow throws up, and I noticed he wasn't making much progress. For 10 minutes I watched, but the pile never seemed to shrink.

This puzzled me, for certainly he was going at it with great gusto.

Then I looked at his shovel, his weapon of choice.

Plastic.

Oh, my. That is the height of pitiful.

Anyone who would use a plastic shovel to shovel snow is someone who ought to live in Florida. If you live in Michigan, even down here in the banana belt of Michigan, you certainly ought to have the sense to go with steel.

Plastic is for milk jugs, credit cards, TV set cabinets. It's not for shovels. Shovels, real shovels, are made of steel. And not that thin, wimpy, '90s sort of steel, but steel so thick and heavy that you can hardly lift the thing. Coal-shovel type steel.

I know whereof I speak. I don't mean to brag - that's a lie, by the way - but I am a shoveling ar-teest, coming as I do from a shoveling culture.

I sometimes shoveled three times a week during the winter months (November through May) when I was a lad growing up in the Upper Peninsula. At the time, I hated it because it was forced labor. My dad, no fool, figured what's the point of having five sons if not to do the grunt work?

But over time, as happens so often with the disciplines of our youth, I came to love shoveling as I grew older.

Therefore, watching someone shovel badly and with the wrong equipment sets my teeth on edge.

Most people think you can shovel any old way. That is true. You can. If you're an amateur hack cretin who doesn't give a damn about anything.

But good shovelers - the pros - know there is an art, an order, a zen, if you will, to shoveling. They don't just go out and flail away willy-nilly. They go out there with a plan and they stick to it.

Mine goes like this:

First, clear a strip down the center of the driveway, beginning at the garage door and continuing on down to the end.

Then return to the top of the drive and with long but sharp strokes, push-flick the snow to the side from the middle.

Do this for 10 feet or so, then go back to the beginning and scoop-lift the snow you pushed to the edges of the drive onto the banks.

Then do the next 10 feet, and so on down to the street.

When you get to the aforementioned furrow at the end of the drive, the game plan changes. For there ... well, there, my friends, is where the bad snow lies. End of the driveway snow requires not the finesse of regular driveway snow but raw, brute force. You can't push this snow. You must heave it. Treat it gently, and it will break you, as it has broken so many before.

I suggest - and you would be wise to heed me - taking medium-sized bites of it. Don't dig your shovel down to the pavement and try to lift entire chunks. Even if you succeed, you'll last only a few heaves before you exhaust yourself.

Pace yourself. Moreover, enjoy yourself.

And in name of all that is decent and true, use a steel shovel, wouldja?

¬January 10, 1999

Ah, the life of a Yooper

Being a Yooper myself, I always thought the true test of Yooperhood was whether you knew the difference between pasties and pasties.

The words are spelled alike, but mean very different things.

A pass-tee is a delectable Upper Peninsula treat consisting of rutabagas, potatoes and a meat of varying origin and quality wrapped inside larded dough.

Whereas pay-stees are what down-state strippers wear to cover their money-makers. (In the U.P., incidentally, strippers have been known to use pass-tees as pay-stees. Drives the hunters wild.)

Anyway, how wrong I was. It turns out that you are a Yooper if you recognize yourself in the "You might be a Yooper if ..." list below.

This is my second such list. The first one, published several months ago, was sent to me by a former newspaperman who thought I'd get a kick out of it, which I did.

Today's list - written by Lord knows who, in true Internet fashion - came via e-mail from a gentleman named Phil Block, who has a web site called Phil Block's U.P. Page. Phil also thought I would get a kick out it, which I did.

So I thought you might, too.

You might be a Yooper if ...

You think the phrase "To open a can of worms" means "we're going fishing!"

People in Wisconsin act superior to you.

Your kid aces the third grade on his ninth try.

You view working the drive-thru window as an important career advancement.

You only know Ted Nugent for his archery equipment.

You think the seven basic food groups are a six-pack of Stroh's and a bag of Doritos.

You saw a sign that said "Drink Canada Dry" and you've been trying ever since.

You think that the Board of Education is the plank the teacher whomps your butt with.

You think the sign in every bar that says NO MINORS SERVED is occupationally biased.

You think the sign saying FINE FOR PARKING means this is a really good spot to leave the car.

You consider membership in the Michigan Militia as a viable military career.

Your junior high had a mandatory class titled "Chainsaw Operation and Repair."

You know 37 ways to prepare meals from roadkill.

Your idea of deer hunting is driving down the logging roads in your 4-wheel drive without your gun.

When sent for a jack, you bring back a fifth of Lynchburg, Tennessee's finest.

Your mosquito repellent doubles as your aftershave.

Your ice fishing shanty is nicer than your house.

You think "ice beer" is leaving a six-pack of Old Milwaukee outside overnight.

Indoor plumbing is something you want to have someday.

You consider a thunderstorm a drive-thru car wash.

Your wife's new fur coat came from animals you trapped yourself.

You think Barney Rubble deserves an Emmy as best supporting actor.

You think algebra is a type of woman's underwear.

You use sheep to mow your lawn.

Nothing in your living room clashes with your stuffed moose head.

Your local bowling alley has six lanes so there's no waiting.

People admiring your earth-tone carpet suddenly realize it really is the earth.

The county library has one book, "Dick and Jane."

The local record store still has brand new 8-track tapes for sale.

You think a Laundromat is something soft to kneel on when you wash your clothes in the creek.

The local movie theater is offering "Gone With The Wind" as a first-run feature presentation.

The local doctor is also the veterinarian, auto mechanic and school bus driver.

Your friends give you a really cool nickname, like "Stinky."

You fertilize the lawn by letting the cows out of the barn.

You burn your kid's statistics textbook as pornography. After all it had an entire chapter on standard deviations.

–October 20, 1997

Holy Wuh! Yooponics is here

Moon Dimple, my boyhood pal and current owner of the world-famous Motel 5 (which is one step down from a Motel 6 in that they don't leave the lights on for you, considering it a waste of money) just outside of Escanaba, our hometown in the Upper Peninsula, asked me about this Ebonics controversy the other day.

"You're telling me that that school district out in California is going to get federal money to teach teachers how to understand black street talk?"

"The term is African Americans these days," I replied.

"And, yes, I believe the district is asking for money from a federal bilingual program."

"Bilingual? You mean street talk is now a separate language, like French?"

"It would seem so."

"Well, ain't that a kick in the pants?" he said. "So do you think they'll get it?"

"What, the money? I don't see why not," I said. "Remember, this is the same government that once bought $10,000 toilet seats."

Moon smiled the same smile I remember him smiling whenever the incredible Mary Jo Pellonpaa wore her world-renowned knit halter top to school way back when.

"All I can say is, God bless America," Moon said.

This was an unusual response. Moon typically takes a dim

view of government in general, government handouts for special interests in particular.

"Why are you so happy?" I asked suspiciously.

"Because," he said, beaming.

"Because why?"

"Because I'm going to be a rich man."

"Oh?"

"Sure, I'm going to get me some of those federal bilingual funds."

"On what grounds?"

"Why, on the grounds that we speak a different language up here in the U.P., of course."

"Different language? What are you talking about?" I said.

"You know, Yooponics."

"Yooponics?"

"Yeah, you know. The way Yoopers speak. We've always had a different way of saying stuff."

"It's not that different," I protested.

"Sure it is!" Moon replied. "For instance, do you think someone from the Lower Peninsula, or anywhere else for that matter, would know what a Yooper is talking about if he said, `Get your chook, Toivo, and we'll go yank some lakers."

"Probably not."

"See, but a Yooper knows that means, Locate your stocking cap, my good friend, and we shall go fishing for lake trout. Or how about this: Holy wuh, da Pack is awesome, eh? You think anyone who doesn't live here knows what that means?"

"I highly doubt it."

"Right. But a Yooper knows it means, Goodness gracious, the Green Bay Packers are a wonderful football team, are they not? Or how about this: Gitcher choppers, we'll shag a Chevy, go Shopko and gitta ice spud. That's gibberish to most people, right?"

"It's almost gibberish to me," I said.

"You've been away too long, my friend. It means: Locate your mittens and we shall grab onto the back bumper of a car traveling on an icy road and slide all the way down to the department store to purchase a metal pole used to make a hole in the ice for ice fishing."

"Ah, yes."

"See?! We got us a whole different language up here. And I

figure if the government is going to be handing out money for people who talk Ebonics, there's no way they can turn down people who want money for speaking Yooponics."

"Holy wuh," I said. "I think you may have a point there, eh?"

"I know," he replied. "Holy wuh, eh?"

–January 13, 1997

How to speak Yooper in one easy lesson

I know what you're thinking.

You're thinking: "I want to vacation in the Upper Peninsula this year. But I wish I had a handy reference guide to the lexicon and dialects of the U.P. so I will know what the heck the guy at the Shell station in Manistique is talking about when he grumbles about how he should go store and get nips, choppers and a chook because he's freezin' his niblets off standing dere pumpin' gas for all da trolls and appleknockers up in da area yankin' lakers and slammin' brewskis, eh?"

Wish no more. The following guide is your salvation. It was compiled largely from the work of Zacharias Thundy and Stewart Kingsbury, English professors at Northern Michigan University in Marquette who studied the Finnish-Cornish-German-Italian-Canadian stew that makes up language in the U.P. But I have added a few words and phrases from personal experience, as I was raised a Yooper and remain proud of my heritage.

I hope you find it useful:

Trolls and appleknockers - Derogatory terms for those living under the bridge, meaning downstaters.

Go store, go movie, go fair, etc. - Yoopers eliminate the "to" in sentences because many of dem are of Finnish descent and Finns don't use prepositions.

Dem, dere, dat - Them, there, that. Again, the Finns don't

use da "th" sound. Which is why you don't see too many of them named Theodore. Eodore sounds kinda stupid.

Pasty - It's pronounced pass-tee, not pay-stee. A pay-stee is what the girls at the strip joint wear. (Or so I've heard.) Word of caution: If it ain't got rutabagas, it ain't a true pass-tee.

Cow pasty - You eventually step in one of these if you spend time around a farm or City Hall.

Chit - Ditto.

Holy wuh! - That means wow, golly or holy chit.

Chook, choppers, nips - Stocking cap, mittens, socks.

Lakers - Lake trout, the national fish of the U.P.

Favre - Pronounced Farve. He's our quarterback, of course. What, you missed the Super Bowl?

Pank - Pank is what you do when you flatten down snow. You pank a lot of snow in da Yoop. It's easier than shoveling it.

Shopko - The U.P.'s version of Wal-Mart, albeit without the annoying old guy at the door greeting you.

Smeltin' - The intrepid pursuit of tiny fish that "run" every spring. Usually caught with a garbage can with tiny holes cut in the bottom in one hand and a Stroh's in da other.

Swampers - You wear these when ya go smeltin' so your boots don't get wet.

Squeeky cheese - A traditional Finnish yogurt that takes its name from the sound you emit after eating it.

Youse - As in, "What kin I git youse?" Without the word youse, U.P. waitresses would be unable to communicate.

Sauna - You know what a sauna is, but you probably say it wrong. Up north it's called a sow-na, not a saw-na.

Eh? - This is tacked onto the end of many sentences in the U.P. It does not necessarily mean the speaker is asking you a question. It's merely an expression. It's Canadian, if you must know, eh?

Ya - Means "yes." But "na" does not mean "no." You follow?

Shackin' - I did this as a kid. You grab the bumper (back, if you're smart; front, if you're suicidal) of a car passing by on an icy road and slide along behind it in a squatting position. A standard U.P. myth is the one about the kid who lost his fingers when a car took a corner too fast. It never happened, as far as I know, but if you want to freak out a Yooper parent, hook a pair of those fake rubber hands to his or her bumper.

That's it. I hope this list helps. Now if you'll excuse me, I have to go store, eh?

Oh, and one more thing: Just so you know, niblets ain't corn.

–March 20, 1997

Upnorth living is required living

We're lucky we have an up North.

People in other states, where do they go on vacation? Maybe some of them travel in a northerly direction. Maybe they refer to going up North. But they don't go "up North" in the Michigan sense of the word.

In Michigan, up North should almost be one word. "Where you going this weekend?" "Oh, you know, Upnorth." Like that.

Upnorth is such a distinct place it should be listed on the map. You'll get a lot of arguments on where exactly Upnorth begins, but my take on it is that you draw a horizontal line through Mt. Pleasant. Anything north of that is Upnorth. Anything south is the land of downstate.

Almost all of my vacation time is spent Upnorth. And most of my summer Sunday afternoons are spent on southbound I-75 trying to get home, cursing all the while at the endless and creative reasons that rubbernecking fools find for causing traffic snarls. (Last weekend's reason: two dead deer on the shoulder. "Look, mommy, entrails!")

What they ought to do is build a separate highway for people going to and returning from Upnorth. I'm not kidding. Take a poll. Betcha 90 percent of the electorate would say, "Heck, yeah! Great idea!" I think people would pay extra taxes for a five-lanes-in-each-direction Upnorthway. (When it happens, remember where you heard it first.)

That's how strongly people feel about Upnorth. It's a wonderful, special place. I always feel sorry for people I meet who say, "I've never been up north."

For them, I offer a glimpse of what exactly they're missing. Upnorth is:

• The first smell. For me, it's when I exit the car, breathe deeply and ... aaaah. It's a mix of trees and clean, cool air. Puts me in a good mood instantly.

• The smell of warm pine needles on a hot day. (I'm big on smells.)

• The feel of hot sand.

• Opening dusty cabins for the first time since last fall.

• Anorexically-skinny black squirrels, which we don't seem to have down here. Our squirrels are all gray and fat.

• The Caribbean greens and blues of Upnorth lakes on a perfect sunny day, and the way the sun off the water hurts your eyes, but you can't look away.

• Long days at the beach where the kids forget that they're being tortured by being dragged away from their video games and TV sets.

• Bad food at awful diners that are wonderful for their awfulness.

• Sunburned tops of feet. I know it's finally summer when I get my first patterned case of sandal burn.

• Endless games of cribbage or Monopoly or backgammon with family or friends that are so much fun you wonder why you never play at home.

• Fruit stands. Wonderful, wonderful fruit stands.

• Tiny, distinct villages that are such a marvel to those of us who live in the amorphous, everyplace-is-one-place towns and suburbs down here.

• The view from the top of an honest to goodness hill. (We don't have many hills in the land of downstate. You ever notice that?)

• Sand dunes. We take our dunes for granted. I tried explaining a sand dune to someone from Tennessee once. They looked at me like I was crazy.

• Something we're darned lucky to have.

¬June 11, 2001

Me,
Myself
and I

Here it comes - the big 4-0

I am making a list and checking it twice.

Drive across country to "find" self.

Open chi-chi bed and breakfast.

Become one with universe.

Buy ridiculously large motorcycle, grow beard, join Hell's Angels.

But nothing seems right. Especially that beard thing. (Still can't grow one.)

See, I'm about two months shy of turning 40. Some people, when they approach that milestone, calmly reflect on the past and make modest, dignified goals for the future realizing the whole time that they probably won't reach those goals because, hey, that's life.

Me, I'm planning to have a MAJOR mid-life crisis.

Start a dotcom company.

Move to Key West, open oyster bar.

Cattle drive!

I know, I know. How utterly predictable. Guy faces middle age. Guy freaks out. Guy does something ridiculous. But give me some credit here. I'm not going to do something ridiculous. I plan on doing something ridiculous AND embarrassing. And stupid. Possibly fatal.

Fly to England, solve crop circle thing.

Attempt to raise Titanic by hand.

Learn to rap.

(Hey, I 've got rhythm. I could be Puff Daddy, and in my case, the name actually would mean something because I AM a daddy. Word to you, suckah!)

I know how pathetic this must seem, but I can't help it. Some people - I think they're called optimists - view life in terms of things they've done. When they turn 40, there's this feeling of warmth and accomplishment. Me, I'm the opposite. My view of 40 is more along the lines of: "OHMYGOD, I'M ALMOST DEAD AND I HAVEN'T DONE ANYTHING YET!"

I mean, what the hell HAVE I been doing these past 40 years? You'd think I'd have more to show for 40 years on this planet than a great job, a wonderful wife and three beautiful children. That's it? What a waste!

Where's the million dollars I was supposed to have by now? Where's the exciting career as a race car driver or astronaut or business tycoon? How come I'M not Tiger Woods? I want my Nobel Prize, dammit!

Anyway, my thinking is that if I do something major for my 40th birthday, that'll be the jolt I need to continue doing major stuff for the rest of my life.

I've considered some grand symbolic gesture:

Solve Israeli-Palestinian thing.

I've thought about major life changes:

Move to small Bahama island, name self king.

Write great American novel, turn down Pulitzer as "too commercial."

Win multi-state lottery; buy Iowa.

I've considered epic one-time adventures:

Climb Everest ... naked!

Hike the Appalachian Trail ... naked!

Learn to dive bomb ... naked!

I've even asked my wife. (Her view: "You want adventure, angst-boy? Something totally new? How about learning how to operate the washing machine?")

Honestly, nothing feels right. Which is where you come in: Plan my mid-life crisis. Please. I'm beggin' ya. Send me your suggestions. I'll pick one, try it and give you full credit, which means my wife will be calling you hopping mad, so you might want to keep that in mind.

One thing, though. I am NOT joining the WWF.

I look terrible in Spandex.

–March 21, 2001

I hereby resolve to ... live

Today I am 40. In my time, I have lived and I have not. I have witnessed more sunsets than I can count. But I have more fingers and toes than the number of sunrises I have seen.

Therefore, I hereby resolve to wake the heck up earlier more often. The grace of the world is most evident at dawn. I shall not miss it.

I have become a fair to not-completely-embarrassing athlete in middle age. But I never played for the Detroit Tigers or even made the high school baseball team, which is something I wanted to do more than breathe.

I hereby resolve to forgive myself for never being quite good enough. (If only they had creatine back then.)

I have trekked the Grand Canyon, toasted Paris from atop the Eiffel Tower and backpacked the spine of California. But I have never smelled the jungles of Costa Rica, dreamed of the past atop the Great Wall of China or witnessed a pride of lions sleeping off the heat of the day on the African savanna.

I hereby resolve to save more money to visit the places of my dreams.

I have learned how to make some kick-tail chili. But out of sheer laziness and the indulgence of others (thank you, ladies), I have never learned how to truly cook.

I hereby resolve to shock my wife and learn how to cook meals that don't include the use of a take-out menu.

I have read widely and passionately - Thoreau, Shakespeare, Steinbeck, Harrison and others. But I have never myself tried to write the great American novel. Or even a so-so American novel.

I hereby resolve to swallow my self-doubt (the most important skill in life, I figure) and give it a go. (What the heck. At least once in a life, a person ought to throw a Hail Mary pass.)

I have learned to type really fast. But I never have played the piano, another thing I have always wanted to do.

I hereby resolve to spend less time on these keys and more time on those keys.

I have developed a number of very close friends. But I also have held most other people at arm's length, mostly out of bashfulness, a distaste for small talk and an inability to remember the name of people I've just been introduced to.

I hereby resolve to step beyond myself and try to get to know people, not just because I'm missing out on a lot, but also because, hey, who wants a sparsely attended funeral?

I have driven responsibly my whole life. But I never have had the rush of red-lining an automobile.

I hereby resolve to find an empty, straight road someday and let 'er rip. Just once.

I have conquered many fears, including a fear of heights, a fear of failing and a fear of speaking to large groups of people. But since childhood, I've never once swam underwater because of a childhood accident.

I resolve to swim the length of a pool under water, then celebrate with ridiculously expensive champagne. One should celebrate the death of one's fears, even the little ones.

I have done many things in my life. But I also have done very little. I hereby resolve to take more chances, have more "have dones" and fewer "have nots."

In whatever time remains to me, I hereby resolve to live.

–May 16, 2001

My dirty little secret

I am going to tell you something that is really going to tick you off if you are a married female.

I know it's going to tick you off because it severely ticked off the two married females to whom I first said it here at the office. See, we were standing around chatting when the conversation turned to laundry. Why laundry? The only thing I can figure is that someone mentioned the ocean and that led to someone mentioning the tide and that reminded someone else of the detergent - you know, Tide - and that got us going on laundry. (Yes, we'll talk about anything. Tides. Prostates. Sometimes even work.)

Anyway, I nonchalantly said, "You know, I've been married for almost 15 years and I've never once done the laundry."

There was a stunned silence.

"By 'never' you mean 'seldom,' right?" asked one of them, the smile drifting from her face.

"No, never," I said. "Ha, ha, isn't that something?"

"He's just kidding you," said the other woman. "I mean, in 15 years he'd have to have done it ONCE. Otherwise he'd be, like, this TOTAL clod."

Failing to recognize that this was my opportunity to lie like a rug then change the subject, I blathered blithely on.

"No, honestly. Never washed. Never dried. Never folded.

My wife's always taken care of it."

There was more stunned silence, followed by more of me happily zipping through warning signs.

"In fact, I don't recall ever doing it before I got married either. In college, my girlfriends or the neighbor girls always did it. And before that my mom did it. So, now that I think of it, I've NEVER done laundry."

Their faces said the following: dirt ball.

But what can I say? I was popular with the girls in college, because I was one of those guys thought to be a "good listener." So they were always willing to throw my laundry in with theirs. My mom, bless her heart, was raised in a time when there was a strict division of labor between the sexes.

And my wife? Well, the lovely yet formidable Marcia, a woman who makes Gloria Steinem seem like Rush Limbaugh, won't let me touch the laundry.

"You'll wreck it," she says. "Go mow the lawn."

She knows whereof she speaks. Once, early in our marriage, in a sudden and inexplicable fit of helpfulness, I decided to break my streak and attempt the laundry.

So I grabbed the hamper and headed for the basement. Once there, I opened the washer, dumped in the clothes - all of them, lights, darks, jeans, Marcia's new white blouse - and turned the dial to permanent press. (I figured, "Permanent. Huh. Sounds pretty good.")

Then without reading the instructions on the box of detergent - I'm a guy; guys know that instructions are for saps - I shook in what I would conservatively estimate was a half pound or so. (I figured, as guys are wont to do, that more was better.)

My hand was on the dial to turn on the machine when a voice said, in harsh, clipped tones: "What. The heck. Do you think. You're doing?"

Marcia.

"Doing the laundry," I said innocently. "Aren't you proud of me? Here, let me turn this here dial and. ..."

She hissed: "Just back. Away. From. The machine."

And she's never let me near the washer again. So, you see, it's not my fault. I would love to do the wash, but. ...

When I told this story to the women at the office, one of

them asked, "Be honest, did you do all that incredibly stupid stuff on purpose so you could get out of having to do the laundry ever again?"

Moi?

–August 31, 1998

Storms just blow me away

The sky turned the color of a bruise. The wind picked up. Kids were hustled inside by their mothers. The flag out front writhed and popped.

Thunderstorm.

My kind of weather.

I love thunderstorms. I love blizzards. I love wind storms. I love extreme weather of any sort. My dream is to someday watch a tornado snake toward me. I would be like that geek on the home video shows: "Look at that, honey! Wow, it's great! Comin' right at us! Whoo, man! I'm going out on the porch and ..." FWOOSH! (Voice trailing off as he is sucked into the sky on his way to Oz): "AAAAaaaahhh!"

One of my favorite memories of childhood is a wind storm that blew over a huge oak on the next block, which smashed a house in two. The girls in the neighborhood tsked about how sad it was for the family that lived there. All the boys wondered what it would be like to be inside a house when a tree fell on it.

I've also always wanted to drive a sled team in the Yukon during a blizzard with the steam from my breath icycling my mustache and beard (I don't have a mustache and beard, but for a good blizzard I'd grow one).

I think it's a guy thing. My wife is horrified at my fondness for bad weather. She always knows where to find me when a storm hits. I'll be on the front porch, my nose sniffing the air like a collie for the marvelous and possibly completely imagined smell of electricity.

We had a real doozy a couple of weeks ago. Thunder, lighting, sideways rain.

I immediately flipped to the Weather Channel, which is command central for guys during bad weather. It's the first place we tune to. What I like is that you can tell the guy announcers are loving it, too. They try to be serious and professional and "concerned," but you know that if they could they'd be rubbing their hands together and saying stuff like, "Hoo boy! Check this out! Hail the size of ripe melons!"

At one point they issued a severe weather advisory. Conditions were right for a tornado. Marcia's reaction: "Maybe we should take the kids down to the basement." My reaction: I strode out to the front porch to get a gander.

"You're nuts," Marcia said.

"Come witness the wrath of the gods, my love!" I roared, the wind carrying off my words like leaves. "Rage, angry gods! Rage on!"

The day after, we were standing with a group of friends when the lovely yet formidable Marcia brought up the storm and my fascination with it. One of the women sighed. She said: "That's how my husband is, too. His big dream is to chase a tornado in his truck." She said this in the sort of tone you'd use to describe a dog who keeps getting into the trash.

Listen, I can't explain it. I'm not sure why men love storms. Perhaps it's the power thing. We love the swift and violent employment of awesome power, even if it tears the shingles off the roof.

Or perhaps it's that men never grow up. We start out liking loud, noisy, violent things, and no matter how civilized we grow to be on the outside, the little boy inside of us still responds to a good lightning strike by saying, "Cool!"

Or maybe it's a primal thing. Maybe the cave men liked storms. Maybe during storms the cave women didn't make the cave men go out and hunt stuff that could eat them, and they got to stay home for some afternoon delight.

Well, it's possible.

–May 22, 2000

The tie revolution has begun!

Members of the resistance, take heed: At last, he is come.

I am speaking here of Prince Claus of Holland, my friends.

He is the one for whom we have long waited. He is the one who shall lead us to the promised land, where a man's neck, yearning to breathe free, is at last unbound from the evil that is the necktie.

He emerged, as all messiahs do, suddenly and in the strangest location, in this case a fashion show in Amsterdam, the Netherlands.

In a speech to open a show of African fashion, Prince Claus stepped to the podium, looked silently at the audience, then yanked off his navy blue necktie and threw it at the feet of his wife, Queen Beatrix.

He then snarled the words we all have snarled in secret lo these many years: "A snake around my neck."

Immediately, members of the local resistance came out of hiding. The first was a TV newscaster who was reporting the story. When he finished, he ripped the tie from his neck as a show of solidarity. This inspired the sportscaster to do likewise. And this inspired viewers galore, one of whom told a newspaper: "A necktie is like a dog leash - both symbolize a limit on freedom!"

Yea, verily.

of Holland is suddenly afire with the lust for Windsor-knotless necks. In Internet chat rooms, Hollanders are calling Claus' action "the Declaration of Amsterdam." Others have dubbed the growing fear and loathing of neckties "Claustrophilia."

The fire is even beginning to spread beyond Holland's borders. All across Europe, men are de-noosing themselves, crying "No more! The tie has enslaved our Adam's apples too long!"

Here in America, newspapers everywhere picked up the Claus story.

Could that light the fires of emancipation here?

No one would be happier than me.

I loathe ties. I believe neckties were designed long ago by a woman angry about having to wear corsets.

Women these days continue to buy ties for their husbands, boyfriends, fathers and brothers because they're ticked off about high-heeled shoes and unequal pay. (And because, OK, guys annoy the hell out of them, but that's another story.)

A tie, in my view, is a useless piece of cloth good only for displaying either your incredible lack of taste or your rotten aim with soup.

I have boycotted ties for years. I refuse to wear them to anything other than a funeral or a wedding (which, too often, turn out to be one and same).

I have left strict instructions with my wife that when I die I am not to be buried in a suit and tie. I don't want to spend eternity pulling at my collar.

And I won't, unless I write too many bad columns and am sent south instead of north. In Hell, I am convinced, the devil makes men wear ties all day, every day. And probably corsets, too.

There are medical reasons, as well, for my aversion to ties.

As Claus noted, ties are a snake around a man's neck. And not just any snake, but a boa constrictor, growing ever tighter until oxygen can no longer get to the brain.

The result is seriously impaired judgment. And in case you doubt me, Ken Starr wears ties all the time, probably even to bed. I rest my case.

It is indeed a sweet day. I have waited many moons for the

anti-tie movement to begin. At last the moment is upon us.

The leader is here, my brethren! The day of liberation nears! We shall overcome the tyranny of the tie, one knot at a time.

With liberty and free breathing for all.

–December 21, 1998

Living in
fear of
the phone

I have lived in fear of the phone for nearly eight years now.

My father, Joe, died June 10, 1993, after playing in a softball game. His body was 60, his spirit much younger. It was too soon.

I can still hear the ring of the phone that night. It was late. Just late enough that you immediately know that something has happened somewhere to someone you love. We had a tan, squat, sit-on-the-table phone at the time, the kind with the actual ringer inside and the huge, heavy handset.

I can still feel the heft of it in my hand. I can still hear my mother's voice in my ear - low and trembling as she gave me the news. And I can still feel - am in fact feeling right now as I write this - what it was like, that punched-gut feeling, the horrible churn of fear and pain and disbelief. My father gone? It couldn't be. Other people's fathers die. Not mine. Not mine.

Since that night, each time the phone rings I relive a slice of that feeling. Maybe I have "issues," maybe I'm just scarred, but I can't help it. I hold my breath a little each and every time, releasing it only when it turns out to be someone wanting me to switch long-distance companies or a friend of my son's wanting him to come over to play or my mom calling to ask when I'm coming home for a visit.

Years of those wonderful, ordinary, stuff-of-life calls had muted the voice of my fear, to the point where it was just a tiny whisper deep inside, almost inaudible. But a call out of place - a little too late, a little too early - would always cause it to find its full voice once again, and it would shout, "Brace yourself, this could be it. Your brother, your mother, your child."

Then the phone rang just a little too early Monday morning. I was in bed, half asleep. My wife, Marcia, answered, listened for a moment, then gasped and put a hand to her mouth. My stomach knotted and I threw back the covers and went to her as she listened, shaking.

This time it was her father, a warm, witty man I've been lucky to have for a father-in-law the past 17 years. He had a heart attack up north, her near frantic mother informed her, and was at that moment being flown by helicopter to a hospital in the city 40 miles away. Marcia got all the details that she could, hung up then buried her head in my chest.

It is Tuesday now. She is off to see him. I am at home with the children. She didn't want them to see their beloved Papa the way she knew he would be. She didn't want them to be frightened. Plus, now is the time for her to be a daughter, not a mother.

So she grabbed a few things and went. So flustered was she that she walked out without the bag she had just moments before packed. Noticing, I called her back and she gave me a smile and a shrug as if to say, "Nothing's right, is it?" Oh, damn, no. Nothing is. Once again, with the ring of a telephone, life has that turned-on-its-ear quality to it. Reality has returned after a few years of leaving us alone, time in which we again had fooled ourselves into believing that nothing bad happens in this life.

Will he be all right? Right now it looks good, from the dribs of information I have. He spent the first day in intensive care, throwing up blood. By this morning, his nausea had passed, his blood pressure dropped toward normal and his color returned. His heart is too bruised to operate right now, so no one knows what the future holds.

I do know that he murmured his opposition to Marcia dropping everything and rushing to see him. "She's coming up this weekend anyway," he said, or something to that effect. Grumbling is always a good sign, isn't it?

I'm choosing to believe so, as I sit here within arm's reach of the phone, hoping for once that the next time it rings and my breath catches and I am fearing the worst, as I have for years and years now, that the news instead is good.

–April 11, 2001

Honored to stand in for dad

My sister and I are in line, waiting for our turn to walk down the aisle.

I am giving her away, which is funny because as a kid I used to joke about giving her away, usually to a pack of gypsies.

That's how brothers and sisters are, right? That's how we were, anyway. Fought like cats and dogs.

And now look at us.

She's in a hand-made gown of white. A dress. My tomboy sister. The last time I saw her in a dress was at the funeral.

And me. I'm in a tuxedo, looking for all the world like a penguin with a green plaid vest.

We are both smiling. We are both proud. It's a happy day. And yet I can't stop thinking: "Man, I wish I weren't here."

The line advances. The first of six bridesmaids heads down the aisle with her penguin escort. I glance over at my sister. She has the radiant, nervous look of a bride-to-be.

In her eyes I see a shine that says this is the crowning moment of her life to date. I know she's happy that I'm the one giving her away.

But I also know she's thinking the same thing I am: "Man, I wish he weren't here."

This was Dad's job, his honor, her dream. But he died - what? - four years ago now? It can't possibly be that long.

He never said so, but she was his jewel. They had that bond unique to fathers and daughters. His first name, Joe, is her middle name feminized, Jo. That's how close they were.

They were even together when he died. It was at the A&W. He'd gone there after a softball game. She'd stayed behind at the field. He collapsed. Someone ran to get her. She dashed back, watched as the paramedics worked on him. They worked a long time. But she told me later she knew he had already left by the time she reached him.

You could tell a piece of her died with him. So last night at the rehearsal dinner I gave her a locket with his picture in it and "Dad" inscribed on the back. I said: "I feel like I'm a poor substitute."

She teared up and thanked me. My eyes moistened - that's as much as they do - and I said you're welcome. It helped us both a little bit.

It's almost our turn now. She gives my arm a squeeze of relief as the ringbearers - my son and two of his cousins, all of them three - make it down down the aisle without somersaults or fingers up noses.

Dad always wanted a girl. He and Mom had five children, all boys, over a span of 10 years. And finally they figured that was it, no more.

Then, six years later, surprise, there she was. Tada!

Her name was Timothy Matthew. Really. For several days, that's what the nurses at the hospital called her, since my parents, not expecting a girl - why would they? - hadn't bothered to come up with a female name.

To this day, if her brothers want to irritate her, which we frequently do, we'll say, "Hey, Timmy, you were supposed to be a boy."

We are at the top of aisle now, Timmy and me. We are waiting for our musical cue, a sea of eyes upon us. I feel light-headed. Nerves. I've never liked being in the spotlight. I'm not sure why she chose me. Of all her brothers, I'm probably the least like him.

Perhaps the "who" didn't matter. We all think he's here. In some way. In our hearts, at the very least.

I whisper to Jennifer, "You look beautiful," as I imagine my dad would.

The fanfare begins, the congregation stands. I look at her. She tugs on my arm.

And off into her future we march.

—October 26, 1997

Fashion tips from a fashion plate

'll bet you weren't even aware that American men were
in crisis.

But it's true.

A recent survey by Sears, Roebuck and Co. revealed
that men are experiencing "serious fashion challenges" as we
approach the millenium.

Or as they explain it: "For some men, the trend towards
relaxed dress codes and more freedom of expression through
fashion poses more of a challenge than an opportunity -
particularly for those who have routinely depended on a
narrow set of rules to help them dress each morning."

What they're talking about are suits and ties. For years,
all a man had to do to get ready for work was reach in the
closet and find a suit and tie with non-clashing soup stains
and go. It was a bland, boring look, but guys had little choice
because of office dress codes.

Then, for whatever reason, many offices began lightening
up, and in came the concept of "casual Fridays."

I think this is a good thing. I have long contended that
people are more productive if they are comfortable.

After all, since casual Fridays began the stock market has
gone up and up, and we are currently enjoying the longest,
strongest bull market in history. Coincidence? I think not.

But, as the survey says, many men are flummoxed by the

new casualness. They don't know what to wear and what not to wear. They don't know the subtle differences that separate "just-right casual" from "homeless casual."

Perhaps I can be of some help. I come from a long line of relaxed-look fashion pioneers.

My daddy - Casual Joe we called him - was the originator of the guy-with-a-hairy-back-wearing-a-tank-top look that continues to be so popular.

And his daddy before him - Casual Joe Sr. - pioneered the loud striped shirt with loud plaid pants look that has remains a golf course standard to this day.

As for me, back in college I originated the whole Docksiders without socks craze that swept the nation. (Although I do have to admit that it was only because I had run out of clean socks and was too lazy to do the wash.)

I am the also the president of an activist fashion organization called We Don't Care, whose mission is to end job discrimination against those of us who are sartorially indifferent.

So you can see I am uniquely qualified to offer up the following list of fashion dos and don'ts for the man who wants to fit in on casual Friday:

Do: Wear tennis shoes. I wear tennis shoes to the office every day and look how successful I am!

Don't: On second thought, forget the tennis shoes. I just looked at my resume. Maybe Nike was right: It's the shoes.

Do: Throw away all of your ties. I did, all except for one, which has little Green Bay Packers helmets on it. The only time I wear it is when someone dies, marries or, in the case of many of my male friends, both.

Don't: Make cracks about marriage like that in front of your wife.

Do: Consider wearing shorts to the office on hot days. I know. It seems radical. But think about it. Women do it, only they call them culottes, so somehow it's OK. (New name: guyottes.)

Don't: Wear shorts to the office if you work in MY office. I like my lunch right where it is, thank you very much.

Do: Close your eyes when you select pants and shirt from the closet or (in my case) the pile on the floor. The bizarre combinations will dazzle and amuse your friends and co-workers.

Don't: Look in the mirror before heading out the door in the morning.

Trust me. It's better that way.

–May 31, 1998

My suburban conversion is complete

I was telling a friend about the weeds growing in the cracks of my driveway when he stopped me and said, "Do you realize what's happening here?"

Yes, I said. I'm telling you about my weeds. See, there are these dandelions that ...

"What I meant," he said, "is, do you realize what has happened to you?"

Apparently not, I answered.

"You've become one of them."

One of whom?

"The suburbanites."

Oh, come on.

"No, really. Before you moved out of the city, you'd have made fun of someone who noticed he had weeds growing in his driveway, much less someone who nattered on and on about how to get rid of them."

I was not nattering, I said. I was merely expressing my frustration over the fact that my weed killer has not done what it's supposed to do.

"Yeah, and what were you telling me about before that?"

I believe I was telling you about how my lawn looks better when I angle cut it as opposed to the traditional back and forth horizontal cutting pattern.

"See?" he said.

See what?

"Only suburbanites worry about mowing patterns, my friend. An obsession with the appearance of one's lawn is the first sign of creeping suburbanitis."

That may be so, I said. But I am not obsessed with my lawn.

"Oh, no. Do you fertilize?"

Yes. I believe I recently applied a 32-4-8 nitrogen, phosphorous, potassium weed-and-feed mixture.

"And didn't you tell me that you had a grub problem?"

Well, not me, personally. But, yes, my lawn had a serious infestation of the common white grub. But a shot of diazinon quickly cleared it up.

"And aren't you the one who told me last week that you were thinking about buying an edger?"

Yes. But only because it looks better edged. You wouldn't get a haircut and not get your sideburns trimmed, would you?

"See? You're obsessed. Before you moved out of the city you wouldn't have even known what an edger was, am I right?"

True, but ...

"In fact, if I recall, you used to say that grass was such a bother you were thinking about Astro-turfing your lawn so you never had to cut it again."

True, I said that once. I also talked about paving over my lawn and opening a used car lot. But these days I have to face certain realities. If I don't cut my lawn, the neighbors will get upset.

"See, you care what the neighbors think. That's another sign. You never used to worry about the neighbors. You used to leave your shades open all the time, for crying out loud, and I happen to know you stagger around naked in the morning."

Only to the bathroom and back. If the neighbors don't want their breakfast appetites ruined, they shouldn't peep in my windows.

"That's exactly what I mean. You've changed. You close your shades all the time now, don't you?"

Well, I'm a lot more modest nowadays. That's hardly proof, though, that I've become suburbanized.

"Proof? You want proof? You want incontrovertible proof of

your rampant, runaway suburbanitis?"

Not really. But go ahead.

"Barbecue grills."

What about them? I asked.

"You bought one for your deck recently, didn't you."

Um, yes.

"Regular old blue-collar charcoal? Or gas?"

Uh, gas. But ...

"I rest my case."

Oh my god.

–August 24, 1997

Have a nice day, ya jerk

Rudolph Giuliani, the mayor of New York who is famous for once joking on national television that "We can kick your city's a—!," has announced a campaign to get New Yorkers to be nicer to each another.

Note: They can still be obnoxious to the rest of us who only visit.

Said Giuliani: "I think New York will always be a somewhat more sarcastic and humorous city. But that doesn't mean people have to treat each other in a basically disrespecful way."

Yes it does. As a practitioner of the fine art of sarcasm, I can assure you that sarcasm and disrespect go hand in hand.

But that's just a technical point. His overall idea has merit. In these days of road rage, we should all strive to be kinder and gentler to one another.

Perhaps I will give it a try. I'll admit, I have gotten meaner over the years due to overexposure to many of you who act like - and I say this with love in my heart - major jerkwads.

For instance, the other day I was at a light, waiting for my turn to proceed through an intersection that is one of the busiest and most congested in the county.

That's when I noticed the lady driving a minivan off to my right. Just as the light facing her turned yellow, she edged out into the middle of the intersection.

And that's where she stayed. She couldn't proceed because traffic ahead of her was backed up. She could clearly see this. And yet, not wanting to wait through another light, she deliberately chose to pull forward and block the intersection, meaning I and the people behind me could not continue from the opposite direction when we had the green.

She achieved, through her one selfish act, perfect traffic gridlock. And there we all sat, our blood pressures soaring, through two more lights.

My reaction, as it typically is in such situations, was to flip the finger, then tap out a Morse code message to her on my car horn, something to the effect of "You are an inconsiderate moron and should be locked in a prison with other morons where you can stupid each other to death!"

Perhaps that was a bit coarse of me. The next time I find myself in such a situation I will attempt to be kinder and gentler by prefacing my message about her being a moron with a blast meaning "Excuse me," which, I admit, was rude of me to omit, and ending it with another blast meaning "Thank you very much for your consideration in this matter."

There are other situations in which I could improve.

For instance, the other night the phone rang during dinner, and the voice said, "May I speak to Mr. Heller?"

I was immediately suspicious. No one calls me Mr. Heller except people who want to sell me something.

"This is Mr. Heller," I said. Sure enough, it was a long distance phone company creature promising me "big savings" if I would switch.

Now, my normal reaction to such phone calls, is to hiss something to the effect of "Big savings this, pal!" and slam the receiver down hard in hopes of rupturing the caller's eardrums.

I see now how juvenile and thoughtless that was of me. I could have broken the phone, meaning I would have to buy a new one, which would probably make the phone company happy, not to mention endangering the family budget.

What I should have done was use an air horn, the kind employed by obnoxious fans at football games, to try and damage his hearing.

But, hey, I'm new to this nicer stuff. Give me time, I'll do better.

Now go have yourself a nice day.

And I really don't mean that.

–March 2, 1998

Ball drop
a real
let-down

Call me Mr. Excitement, but my New Year's Eve celebration usually consists of sitting around the house with my family playing board games and watching Dick Clark and his wonderful, ridiculous ball.

There are three reasons for this:

One, I'm not much of a party guy. I've always despised small talk. There's a reason they call it that, and that's why I hate it. Invite me to a party where there are scheduled, timed debates on Thoreau, Greenspan or, heck, even that computer-generated first-down line they put into football games now, and I'm there. Invite me to a party where the point is to mill around with people I hardly know and pretend to be fascinated/fascinating, and, I'm sorry, I'd rather stay home and clean my toenails.

Two, despite serious attempts back in college and a few times since, I'm not much of a whoo-hoo kind of guy either. Whoo-hoo guys are the ones at parties, sporting events or concerts who randomly and frequently bellow "WHOO-HOOOO!" to communicate to those around them that: A) they have consumed copious amounts of alcohol, and B) they are major wild partiers who are having an awesome time, dude.

Three, I am flat-out fascinated by that ball in Times Square and equally fascinated with the world's fascination with it.

Think about what a bizarre way this is to mark the passing of another year - tens of thousands of people stand cheek to jowl in the freezing cold for hours to watch (or not watch, since I imagine most of the people who crowd the Times Square area even see the ball because of other buildings) a gigantic lighted ball of steel tubes gussied up like a Vegas showgirl - a ball with no symbolic, religious, cultural or historical significance whatsoever - slide slowly down a pole. Then there's a collective "Whoohoo!" at midnight. Then that's pretty much it.

It's such an odd custom, that no matter where I am or what I'm doing on New Year's Eve, I always find my way to a TV set at midnight to watch the ball and the people in NYC who are so entranced by it. And every year I turn to my wife and say, "You know, maybe we ought to go there one year, just to experience it."

She usually says, "What would you want to do that for? You don't even know anybody who's ever been there."

I do now. My buddy Jim was there this year.

His report: "Well, most people get there at least four or five hours early. And once you're there, it's pretty tight. You're sardines. They put you in these little pens and you're stuck there for four or five hours. There's no music or entertainment except at the end. There's no toilets. And you're not allowed to have alcohol. If you get caught with it, they kick you out."

So what do people do if they can't drink and can't go anywhere and are packed in like sardines and there's no place to go to the bathroom and there's pretty much nothing to do and you're freezing cold?

"Well, you talk to each other, look around, try to keep warm. Every hour someone gets on the loudspeaker and you practice counting down."

So as it turns out, the big ball drop is like one big small-talk party with a bit of whoo-hooing at the end.

Think I'll stay home again next year.

January 7, 2001

PHOTO: STEVE KLEEMAN

Andrew Heller is an award-winning columnist for The Flint Journal in Flint, Michigan. His work has appeared in newspapers across Michigan. He was born in downstate Michigan, but was raised a Yooper and remains one at heart, despite a distinct lack of interest in hunting and 8-month winters. He lives in Grand Blanc Township with his wife, the lovely yet formidable Marcia, and their three children, Sam, Annie and Henry.

Special thanks to: my patient editors at the newspaper (Jackie Braun, Cookie Wascha, Jennifer Walkling, Jennifer Kildee and others) who keep me on the straight and narrow; to Paul Keep, the editor of the paper, and Roger Samuel, the publisher, who stand behind me even when I write stuff that gets them in trouble; to my office wife, Rosemary Reiz, who reads my columns before they hit the street and has no problem saying "That's dumb" or, in rare cases, "Hey, that's not bad"; and, of course to the people far and wide who read what I write, without whom I'd be spending my days saying, "You want fries with that?"